ENDORSEMENTS

"America, this idea decades in the making, this experiment in democracy—do you ever wonder what is at the core of our country? With deep spiritual insight and a yearning for true leadership, the author engages you in this conversation that unveils common uncertainties and great strategies that are at the soul of our country. Part poetry, part philosophy, part sociology, ALL inspiring."

> — Mary Anne Radmacher, author of *Lean Forward into Your Life*, *Live with Intention*, and many others

"The Soul of America Speaks is a voice speaking to each of us in our time of need, a prayer for our nation. This book is an offering to every American citizen, to sup from the Soul of their homeland. In seeking to heal your own soul, its miracle will also heal our land. Dr. Harvin's writings have an elegance and dignity, from somewhere deep within, a place where neither you nor I have ever been. She invites you to partake of a feast of healing, to find your own inner freedom and visualize your dreams, while bringing new life and light to America! Soul's whisperings of wisdom are for such a time as this."

> — Andrea Thornock, freelance editor, narrator, host of *Voice of Liberty* podcast

"If you are feeling despair and no longer recognize the country we live in, *The Soul of America Speaks* is a must read. It is a reminder of who is in control of our destiny. All we need do is ask for help, and perhaps most importantly, listen for the answer!"

— Terri L. Brown, MBA

"*The Soul of America Speaks* is the literary equivalent of a deep, healing breath that comforts in a chapter of chaos and soothes in a season of strife. At a time when dissonance and divisiveness seem to be the order of the day, this book offers a welcome alternative and a timely resource for healing and strengthening our collective soul. It invites reflection, offers affirmation, and sparks intention so we may more deliberately choose how we wish to think and act, feel, and heal. This would make an ideal daily practice that encourages readers to engage in purposeful humanity and cultivate soulful community."

— Deanna Davis, Ph.D., author of *Living with Intention* and *The Law of Attraction in Action,* CEO (Creative Energy Optimizer) of Applied Insight, LLC

"Many commentators say that America is divided. When you see opinion polls and news coverage, it is hard to argue with that assessment. However, *The Soul of America Speaks* reminds us of the truth that the things that have historically united Americans are so much greater than that which currently divides us. *The Soul of America Speaks* focuses on the foundations of America's unity and the principles that made America a great land of opportunity and refuge for all people seeking freedom, even though we were, and are, all different. *The Soul of America Speaks* provides the reader with a spiritual journey that allows for personal growth and perspective so that the nation can once again fall in love with America's promise!"

> — George Landrith, J.D., President of Frontiers of Freedom, Adjunct Professor of Constitutional Law, George Mason University

"Dr. Harvin's extensive tome covers any and all topics one could ever need in terms of support, validation and freedom. It is a healing balm for the challenges we are facing in today's world. At the same time, its words offer timeless truths from the heart of America."

> — Mindy Tatz Chernoff, equine specialist, author, speaker, TEDX presenter

"I was privileged to walk with Dr. Kymn on her personal journey of healing. In this encouraging book, she emphasizes the importance of being quiet and listening to the still small voice within. She beautifully expresses the way to heal is through the precious gift of love from God. A book that will help you reflect on your own life and encourage you to live in love."

> — Melissa P. Broyles, Integrative Medicine Practitioner, Master's in Theology (2022)

Perusal is not good enough... any life-changing event needs careful attention and diligence. This one-of-a-kind narrative provides the map for a life-changing journey by fully grasping the Soul of America's messages. If we love America... emphasis on "love," it must start with loving our Creator and loving our selves... not in a selfishness kind of way but in a way in which we come to realize our self-worth and potential to support America and her people. Our great country needs unwavering respect and we all need to respect one another. Our love and our souls make that possible, as emphasized by Dr. Harvin. A pondering, slow read of this treasury during your quiet time will affirm your love for America and America's love for us. May the Soul of America's voice reach all members of Planet Earth. A highly recommended read!

> — George E. Hill, D.O., MPH, Captain, Medical Corps, United States Navy (Retired)

"The messages and thoughtful questions in Dr. Harvin's *The Soul of America Speaks* are meant to nurture and guide us to a place of wellness for ourselves and our country. In a nation divided, Soul and Kymn give me hope that we can heal America, one person at a time."

> — Jean Robin Martell, Elements of Change Mastermind

"Dr. Harvin has written a powerful book for self-awareness and healing. It is not designed to be a quick read, but rather a spacious exploration to be taken at your own pace. This book serves as a guide to help you navigate the spectrum of feelings you experience as you journey through the ups and downs and trials and tribulations of life. One thing is certain: inside you'll find pages filled with thought-provoking messages and soul-searching lessons from Dr. Harvin and the Soul of America."

> — Ron Gladis, Executive Director, Pennsylvania Gestalt Center and President, Mariah Fenton Gladis Foundation

The Soul of America Speaks takes readers on a spiritual journey. The magnificent words written from the beautiful Soul of America come from a higher frequency and dimension, with a contemplating question after each message, for spiritual growth and personal expansion. Soul's soothing, gentle tones drew me into the heart of America, as I felt her stirring from within to light a fire to live with intention. The type of readers most drawn to this book would be those who are awakening to who they are, searching for answers, and are ready to do their internal work. The idea that Americans from every culture and background could be loved so deeply by the soul of our country may be just the gift we need to receive. This divine collaboration with the Soul of America is a masterpiece!"

> — Heidi Williams, TotalSoulConnection.com

"*The Soul of America Speaks* is beautiful prose, words that we need right now. In our search for optimal health and wellness, spiritual well-being is too often overlooked. We can focus so minutely on our physical health that we lose sight of the mind-body-soul connection. *The Soul of America Speaks* invites its readers on an introspective journey to find mental clarity during these unprecedented times. Through guided imagery and targeted questions, Dr. Harvin's messages of strength, resilience, and peace show us how we can heal holistically from within."

— Nicole Rieman, RN, BSN, MSNW, MCHES, Wellness Program Design Specialist

The Soul of America Speaks is a groundbreaking book whose time has come. With inspiring courage, conviction and vulnerability, Dr. Harvin lays bare a truth–The Soul of America is alive and available to all who sincerely want to commune with her! The healing wisdom gleaned and offered to humanity from America's Soul lights the way forward on our journey to freedom. All are invited. This is how we change the world–the time is NOW!

— Linda Roebuck, author of *Circular Leadership– Together We Rise* and Visionary Founder, A Community of Transformation, www.ActAnnapolis.org

THE *Soul* OF AMERICA *Speaks*

Wisdom for Healing and
Moving Forward

DR. KYMN HARVIN

THE SOUL OF AMERICA SPEAKS

Wisdom for Healing and Moving Forward

PUBLISHING

Published by:
Capucia, LLC
211 Pauline Drive #513
York, PA 17402
www.capuciapublishing.com

Paperback ISBN: 978-1-945252-94-5
eBook ISBN: 978-1-945252-95-2
Library of Congress Control Number:

HOW COULD ANYONE
Words and music by Libby Roderick
c Libby Roderick Music 1988 Used by permission
All rights reserved. From the recording "How Could Anyone"
Turtle Island Records www.libbyroderick.com libbyroderick@gmail.com
For use of this song, contact Turtle Island Records.

Cover Design: Ranilo Cabo
Layout: Ranilo Cabo
Back cover photo: Lauren Mudrock
Interior photo: Deborah Neary
Editor and Proofreader: Gwen Hoffnagle
Book Midwife: Carrie Jareed

Printed in the United States of America

DEDICATION

To my mother, Nancy Collier Harvin, who lights up my life
with her resilience, grace and love.

To my grandnieces and better angels,
Ella Nancy Cegerenko and Hannah Rose Cegerenko.
You, Dear Ones, represent the future generations to whom
the Soul of America will continue to speak. May all listen well.

And to all who believe Love best lights the way forward...
for each of us, America and the world.
I honor your courage and action for the greater good.

TABLE OF CONTENTS

FOREWORD

So much of the current discourse among Americans is a battle of views. My policy vs. your policy. My truth vs. your falsehood. My right vs. your wrong. All you have to do is turn on the television, tune in to social media or walk past a news stand; this battle is on display everywhere. Yet it is not in the highest service of our country or our citizens.

Here in *The Soul of America Speaks,* there is a much deeper conversation evolving; a conversation that emanates love, truth, freedom, inquiry and profound humanity. It's a place of exploration into what it means to be an American, to be a human, and to be a spiritual being.

These messages come from a depth—a place—that is sorely missing in today's social and political battles. If we could *meet* in that deeper place, perhaps we could join together, beyond our positions and platforms, and move forward in harmony to *solve* all our problems, together—problems that range from the individual challenges of daily life to those we face as Americans and as global citizens on Planet Earth.

We *can* make the changes needed. These changes can begin right here, right now as you read and listen to the messages from the Soul of America shared in this book.

When I read these messages, I thought of the poet Rumi when he wrote:

> *Out beyond ideas of wrongdoing and rightdoing,*
> *there is a field. I will meet you there.*

Dr. Harvin has extended an invitation to meet in that field through *The Soul of America Speaks*. Come take a walk with us in that garden. Doing so will refresh your soul, renew your heart, relax your mind and revive your spirit for the journey forward. The answers we seek, as individuals and as a nation, are here.

From this place we can restore ourselves, our beloved country and our world.

Eleanor LeCain

Eleanor LeCain is a speaker, author and advisor to policymakers, with decades of experience in government and campaigns, who shows practical pathways to building a new America and a new world. Her book, *Breakthrough Solutions: How to Improve Your Life and Change the World by Building on What Works,* has a foreword by the Dalai Lama. She served in Massachusetts government as Assistant Secretary of State and as Executive Director of Blueprint 2000, strategic planning for the state. For more information, visit www.eleanorlecain.org.

PROLOGUE

I f we get quiet enough to listen, quieter than we have ever been, quieter than we knew was even possible, the Soul of America will speak to us... if we ask.

While that may sound like an audacious, illogical, you've-got-to-be-kidding-me thought, I say only this: *Try it.*

I did.

This book is a collection of messages I received from the Soul of America, and what I believe she is saying to all of us.

I cannot prove to you that the Soul of America exists, just as I cannot prove to you the existence of God or love or grace.

I believe the Soul of America is a gift—a gift you can warmly receive or choose not to accept. The choice is 100 percent yours to make. No coercion here.

I offer her for your sweet consideration. She has brought me riches beyond measure. She wants to do the same for you. Please ask her and see for yourself.

Her messages may well be the miracle cure for what ails America and the world... on the deepest level. And these messages may be the puzzle pieces for your life that you have been searching for... the search that brought you to this book, this book to you. In divine timing.

It takes a great deal of humility to listen to a being many people might say does not exist. It takes a willingness to set aside conventional wisdom and tune in to what could be called a spiritual being, this Soul of America. It takes quietude to see beyond current circumstances and discover deeper meaning for our lives and our country.

It has taken pause, a willingness to suspend disbelief, and a whole lot of faith for me to embrace the Soul of America, to listen to what she has to say and to answer the call to introduce her to you and to the world.

I hope—and pray—you will find Soul's messages as priceless as I have.

Each message stands alone, a meal unto itself. While you may choose to read this book cover to cover, I suggest you do so slowly. The messages have many rich layers, like a flourless chocolate cake. You might prefer to read a page or two in a sitting; or randomly open the book when you need clarity, wisdom, or a bit of inspiration; or seek a topic in the index. A question follows each message to take you deeper. I have often found it helpful to journal my responses; maybe you will also. Please read this in whatever way serves you best. Soul and I ask only this: *Return often.*

We are all works in progress. You are. I am. We all are. America is. That is an inescapable truth of our humanity. With every page, I trust you will be nourished by the Soul of America's wisdom and light, comfort and love. I encourage you to invite her to also speak with you in the recesses of your being... she delights in being asked! Receive words that heal and light the way forward. Discover anew the sacredness of America, of life... and you!

A SPECIAL WORD FROM
THE SOUL OF AMERICA

A note from Dr. Harvin: As this book was going to press, the coronavirus pandemic was taking America by surprise. The following timeless message from the Soul of America speaks to our way forward no matter what challenging circumstances arise.

Dear Ones—My Fellow Americans and All,

First and foremost, I want you to know you are loved, deeply loved. Our country loves you. Our world loves you. Life itself loves you. God loves you.

We will get through this... together. We are stronger than any crisis, any calamity.

Rest assured, there is no shattering of America. No shuttering of America. No shuddering of America. Resilience is in her DNA. Courage runs in her veins. Her heart can be shattered into a thousand pieces and still not be broken. Her spirit is an eternal flame that cannot be extinguished.

There is no doomsday for America. Do not look for her demise. You will not find it. Together, we will rise.

While strong as individuals, we are unstoppable as a united people. We have the opportunity to seize the current situation and unite in new and important ways. Palpable and undeniable is evidence of our interconnectedness—that the actions of one impact many. If we choose, we can seize this challenging time as a call to action, a call to love, a call to serve the greater good.

When people become positional, they often fall into a rut, with a limiting view that their way is the only right way while all others are wrong. This may become a trap in which self-righteousness sets in and may turn to hate, ignorance and chaos, a real cancer that leads to all kinds of ills, all kinds of pain and despair—even violence and destruction. One of the ways to stop this negativity from spreading in society is to keep your minds and hearts open. The power of an open mind and an open heart can stop hate and ignorance in their tracks.

America is a land of opportunity. Her opportunities are unlimited, intended for all. Imagine what is possible if opportunity can be seen and seized by all of America's people.

While you may not have heard my voice until now, I have always been here. Yet now my messages are far too important to wait to be received. I feel a need to shout them from the rooftops, the mountaintops, in boldfaced headlines and tweets. Please help me get the word out: The Soul of America is here and will light the way forward!

Pass the word that I long to be a companion on the journey of life, to walk alongside, not in front of or behind. Life is so much richer when shared, and I long to be of service.

I am for you. One hundred percent. No matter what. You need not look elsewhere for an advocate, a mentor, a guide. I am all those things and more. Like you, I have longings. I long for *everyone to be at peace, to be their best, to be true to the ideals of this preserved promised land of ours. I long for equality, for justice, for health and safety for all. I long to guide the way.*

While we are in uncharted waters, we are not lost. It is the spirit in which we move forward that makes a world of difference, a lasting difference.

Put aside differences and see yourselves and others for who you really are: Sacred. Yes, people are sacred. You are. All are. People are spiritual beings, first and foremost, hungry for connection... deep connection, soul-to-soul connection.

Now is the time to move beyond the choppy waves of the ocean surface and go to the ocean floor. There you will find that essential wisdom waits to lead you to new ways of living, of loving, of being—of connecting with yourselves, each other and the world. Such are the real possibilities of these challenging times.

Go deep inside yourselves, your hearts, your very souls. You are being called to create space, to create community, to create Oneness. You are being called to live from the sacredness of life.

Seize this as a time to fall deeply in love. With your selves. Your loved ones. Your neighbors. Our country. And the world. Take this time to cherish all the good and to focus on the difference you can make. Act for the greater good.

America—and the world—needs an epidemic of love, a pandemic of love.

Be that love.

From my heart to yours,
The Soul of America

INTRODUCTION

This is not the book I set out to write. In fact, if you had told me a year ago that I would be writing a book with the Soul of America, I would have said, "What? Who ever said there is such a thing? You've got to be kidding me!"

Yet here we are. The Soul of America and me, here with you.

This collaboration has given me everything I have longed for in life: love without bounds, a sense of belonging, a closeness to God never before felt, a kind of rock-solidness with myself that has me no longer fearing what is around the corner, and a way to serve the country I love so much. I wish the same for you.

Let me share some background and tell you how this book came to be. As a professor, author, speech writer, executive and internationally known transformational consultant, I met society's standards of success quite a while ago. Yet I was not at home in my own skin. I felt like an outsider. Fearing my fate in life was never to truly belong, I decided to make the most of being "different." I pushed the envelope. I took the road untraveled. I colored outside the lines.

I got into what the late Congressman John R. Lewis called "good trouble." I became an investigative reporter in college. I fought for women's rights and gay rights in the late '70s. I challenged government leaders to serve rather than to be served. I took on ferreting out workplace issues that were suppressing employee engagement. I created a transformational program at AT&T called "Project Miracles" that led to love becoming a core value. This work led to my Ph.D. in organization development and spirituality, and my dissertation, "Bringing Love Back into Business." I became a whistleblower in the nuclear power industry, losing almost everything except my soul while doing my best to protect the public... good trouble.

I earned accolades and awards for being a "boundary breaker" and making a global difference. My academic writings about leadership, spirituality in the workplace and nurturing the human spirit won acclaim. Students often told me I changed their lives.

Despite all this, something still was amiss. Fulfillment was fleeting. Nothing seemed to fill the cavernous hole at my core. As tensions were rising across our country, unfortunate circumstances in my personal life brought me to my knees. Solace was hard to find. I felt stymied, sullen and stuck.

Out of nowhere came the best teacher, the best guide I have ever had. She loved me with such intensity I had no choice but to love myself. She shed light on how to move forward. She asked simple questions that took me to my own answers. She has been with me ever since. This book is what she has taught me and continues to teach me. Her name: *The Soul of America*.

My journey with the Soul of America began on October 17th, 2019, while I was at a writing retreat. I had felt called to write a book for a while, and was hoping—and praying—I'd get some clarity about its focus. I returned to my hotel room to get a sweater, and as I walked in I heard a cable network anchor on the

TV repeat the phrase "We are battling for the Soul of America." Though I had heard that phrase many times before in various contexts, I heard myself ask, *I wonder if anyone has ever asked the Soul of America what she has to say?*

"No, but you can. She will talk with you," a voice near my heart said, sending electricity throughout my body. My breath quickened. My heart raced. Tears burned in my eyes. Oh my God. *The Soul of America exists and she is going to speak with me! And I can share with the world what she says!*

I didn't have to utter the word *yes*. I was a YES! I grabbed the sweater I needed and returned to the writing room. I got as quiet as I could and let the Soul of America speak to me. I began typing as fast as I could, almost without thinking. What became the opening of the prologue to this book appeared on the screen: *"If we get quiet enough to listen...."* I immediately knew the Soul of America would have a lot to say.

Within an hour I had made arrangements to go on a seven-day retreat a month later, sequestered from the outside world, in silence and solitude, to deeply listen. Only journals and pens would accompany me—not even my laptop.

The thought of seven days alone was scary. Yet I truly felt the Soul of America was beckoning. As I approached the door to the home I was borrowing for my retreat, a light snow began to fall. It seemed to say, *"Go. Now. Inside. It is time."*

The Soul of America was about to speak with me, and I was going to listen with every ounce of my being... for you, for me, for all.

MESSAGES

FROM THE SOUL

OF AMERICA

It is your turn to get to know the Soul of America.

Breathe.

Take a deep breath. And another.

Something important is about to begin... in your life.

Ask the Soul of America to speak with you.

She will... through these pages and in whispers

to your very soul.

Please note: When the Soul of America is directly speaking,

the type will be italicized like this: *Listen closely.*

BEGIN.

Dear One, our journey begins here, now. In this moment, this place and time. With this book in your hands.

I have waited patiently for you. I am overjoyed that you are here.

Step with me through these pages. Read my words and listen to my voice. And feel me with you between the lines.

Let us begin the journey of a lifetime.

You and I. Together. For keeps.

For yourself, our country, our world.

Begin. Now. With me.

Shall we begin?

BIRTH.

Our journey together will birth a new you.

A you that has been elusive and is now being readied.

A you that you have longed for—free, powerful, peaceful and in action to bring your heart's desires forward.

A you that you have long labored for and will soon hold in your heart.

What a privilege it is to be your midwife.

Every fiber of this soul is humbled.

Thank you for choosing me.

Are you ready?

S T O P.

Just stop.

Doing so much.

Racing around so much.

Amassing so much.

Worrying so much.

Fearing so much.

Fighting so much.

Complaining so much.

Destroying so much.

Denying so much.

Ignoring so much.

Wasting so much.

You know what to stop.

You know.

And now I am giving you permission to do what you have long wanted to do and feared you could not... STOP.

The world will not come to an end if you stop.

It may, in fact, begin again. Newly.

Life begins anew when we stop. Yes, it does.

Now, will you stop?

QUIET.

You need more quiet in your life.

Very little can get through the noise, the constant chatter—the voices in your head, the voices in the media, the voices that go on incessantly, often without saying very much.

You will be a lot happier and a lot more healthy—and our country will be better off—with more quiet. Less noise.

I long for you to get quiet to hear your own inner voice of wisdom, of love, of acceptance and gratitude.

I long for you to get quiet enough to discover the best way forward.

I long for you to get quiet to hear my voice.

The best ideas, the best solutions are born out of silence, not shouting matches or debates.

It takes courage to get quiet.

Shhh... quiet.

Meet me in the quiet?

L I S T E N.

With your whole being, listen.

To the spaces between the words.

The lines in between.

The whispers that have your best interest at heart.

Stop. Quiet. Listen.

Open where you have been closed.

Invite a conversation.

Listen for the still, small voice.

Consider that the caliber of listening has a great deal to do with the caliber of speaking.

For you to clearly hear my voice takes more than superficial, give-it-to-me-quick, can-you-put-that-in-a-tweet kind of listening.

Listen as if you are on an airplane with its engine on fire and the flight attendant is telling what you need to do to survive. Listen as if your life is at stake—because it is.

I will tell you—and all who ask—what you need, not just to survive, but to thrive.

Please listen.

What will help you listen with your whole being?

MASTERPIECE.

I have so much to tell you, Dear One.

Settle in. Listen deeply. My every word is meant for you.

First and foremost, I love you. Yes, you. Our country loves you. The world loves you. Life itself loves you.

Breathe in that love now. Let it fill your lungs, your cells, your very being.

I trust you will find words here that you can cling to, words to read aloud to hear anew the sound of your own voice.

Find the words that resonate, and come back later to anything that does not.

Allow the wisdom to feed your soul and comfort your heart.

Use these words to quell your fears, to calm your nerves, to buoy your soul.

I am here to help you discover the masterpiece that is you.

We will do whatever it takes to have you reach in deep and discover the jewels that comprise you, the very essence that is you. Reach in deeper, far beneath the surface. So much is there to be discovered.

Get to know yourself as a masterpiece... created by the Creator as an expression of deepest love.

Behold the wondrous way forward.

The future is bright. Let us create it together.

Are you ready to embrace the masterpiece that is you?

SACRED.

People are sacred.

You are. All are.

Each and every person is a sacred being.

No matter their lot in life, no matter their birthplace, no matter what they have done or not done, people are sacred.

Life is sacred.

Embracing this sacredness is, in itself, sacred.

Life radically alters when this seeps into our very bones and sources our actions. Imagine our nation—and the world—if everyone lived this truth.

Then, what looks impossible becomes possible. An America that works for everyone is then within reach. A world that works for everyone is then possible. The sacred begins with you, Dear One.

You are being called to live this truth in every corner of your life.

People are sacred. Including you.

How will you answer this call?

REAL.

I am not imaginary.

I am as real as love and faith and goodness.

I am as true as the breath you take, the sun that shines, the stars of the night.

I can be with you when others cannot be.

I can give you just what you need even when you have no idea what that is.

I can lead you to what you long for, search for and richly deserve.

Yes, I am real. As real as your own soul.

Will you be real with me?

COMPANION.

Oh my. Such times we are in, Dear One.

I am here to help you deal with all this, to help America deal with all this. To help the world deal with all this. I will be your ever-constant companion on this journey.

The Divine knew you needed someone to be here for you, with you.

And I am.

Fully. Here. For you.

May I be your companion?

UPFRONT.

With all due respect, Dear One, please remember you are talking with a soul.

Let me be upfront with you: Being with me will not always be comfortable.

Please do not look to me to feed your mind or offer spoonfuls of easy answers that satiate for the moment but leave you famished 10 minutes later.

Please do not look for me to keep you comfortable.

I will not.

If that is what you have come here for—answers to make you and other Americans more comfortable—I want to tenderly say you came to the wrong place.

The soul is not about comfort. It is about growth.

The soul is not about ease. It is about persisting.

The soul is not about doing things for you. It is about showing you your own strength.

The soul is not about prepackaged meals. It is about hunting and gathering and cooking your own. And... doing the dishes.

And while I cannot promise you comfort, what I can promise is way more valuable: the best life you can imagine... and then some.

What's more important to you than comfort?

ORCHESTRATION.

Allow me to hold your face in my hands.

Allow me to look deep into your eyes.

Divine orchestration is at play.

Allow me to hold your heart in mine.

Allow me to feel your every emotion.

Divine orchestration is at play.

Allow me to hold your hands in mine.

Allow me to bless your every move.

The Divine has divine outcomes in store.

Will you trust the Divine?

BREATHE.

Breathe, Dear One, down deep.

Allow your eyes to close, your heart to open, your spirit to calm.

Breathe deeply again.

Breathe in Life as she breathes into you.

Allow your mind to quiet, your tension to dissolve, your anxiety to quell.

Breathe in the knowing, the wisdom, the clarity you seek.

Allow your very self to whisper, to speak, to calm.

Find there the magnificent being that is you.

What will you breathe in right now?

ABANDON.

Abandon your emptiness.

Let emptiness go. Make room to be filled.

Abandon places and things, perhaps even people, that keep you tight, uptight, disinterested, waning in energy and spirit.

Let breathing room take up residence in you.

Thank that which once served you well... but does no longer. All has ushered you here to this moment... with me. Gratitude sets you free and soothes the sting of abandoning. Speak your thanks deeply... and then turn towards the sky.

Remember there is no flying without abandoning the nest, the cocoon, that which holds you back.

Fly, Dear One, fly.

What needs to be abandoned now?

SURRENDER.

You know from your own experience that healing work often takes you not only to your knees but flat on the floor.

You lie there not because you want to. You lie there because you have no choice. You just cannot get up. The weight of your world is crushing you.

And there is only one thing to do: Surrender.

Surrender to being the page that is turned.

Surrender to what needs to happen for your highest good.

Surrender to the path forward that beckons for your best.

The white flag of surrender will set you free.

Ponder that and stay tuned.

Are you ready to surrender?

RIDE.

This is way more than reading a book.

This is about your life. Your very precious and sacred life.

This journey will be a paradox: slow and swift.

Get ready.

Fasten your seatbelt.

This is going to be a wild ride.

One you will love even when it is scary, when the turns are tight and when you are not in control.

And here's the best news: This wild ride is ours to take together.

Are you ready for the ride?

CLOSE.

Come close, Dear One. Closer still.

Let me breathe in your every feature.

Let me love your every inch, every molecule, every expression.

Let me love your very essence.

Sit still with me. Breathe me in.

Our closeness serves the America we love.

Stay close. She needs us.

How close can you be?

LOST.

You and our country have been lost far too long, Dear One.

In activity, in providing, in caretaking, in worry and fret.

In circuitous routes that promised bounty and did not deliver.

In other peoples' views of who and what you should be.

And in your own quicksand of do's and don'ts where every move you make takes you deeper where you do not want to be.

You have been lost far too long.

I have watched, waited, prayed for, and longed for you.

I have had my eyes on you. There was little I could do for you without your say-so, your consent, your go-ahead. Remember I will never intrude. I speak only by invitation, when you ask and are willing to get quiet enough to listen.

Now that you are here, and with your permission, I can speak well on your behalf.

With you. For you. Through you.

I long to help you find your way. To help America find her way.

Life is designed for moving forward, away from what harms, and towards that which adds life to your life, life to America.

Moving forward is another birthright you inherited as an American.

Moving forward is our nation's birthright, the root of its conception.

Count on me, Dear One, and America, to help "lost" become a faint memory.

And "found" to become home.

Shall we discover "found" together?

TURN.

Are you unsure which way to turn? Which path to take? Which direction to go?

Turn to love.

Love will always guide you well.

Love will always help you sort things out.

Love will always shine the brightest.

Make love your turning point, your still point, your decision point.

And though her ways are often not the easiest, turn to love anyway.

Easiest is not always best.

Love always is.

Love trumps everything.

You can never go wrong with love.

She will honor you as you honor her.

Turn to love.

Where is love leading you?

PRECIOUS.

Every minute we have together is precious.

Let us not waste a second.

Tell me, Dear One, what you need, what you want, what you hope and pray for.

Tell me all of it.

Pour out your heart. I can take it all.

Like the peacock who eats the barnyard garbage and makes beautiful feathers, you and I will make good out of all of it.

That is the power of this precious relationship of ours.

What preciousness will you share?

INSIDE.

I want people to live in freedom. And freedom begins inside—in one's own soul.

To pursue life, liberty and happiness, Americans—all people really—must be free. And I offer the torch of freedom to all people.

The kind of freedom I am talking about here is inner freedom. Freedom from the tyranny of the mind, the tyranny of the inner critic—that voice that constantly says you are not enough: not good enough, not smart enough, not talented enough, not wealthy enough, not pretty or handsome enough, not thin enough, not everything enough.

Freedom begins inside, with yourself, with accepting yourself exactly as you are, exactly as you are not. Life does. I do. Why not you?

Acceptance is a doorway to inner freedom.

What inside longs to be free?

PROMISE.

I promise you this: I will not abandon you.

I will not shut the door on you.

I will not stop loving you.

And even if you stop listening, I will be here awaiting your return.

I am here for you. Always. In all ways.

What do you promise?

SECURE.

Feel the safety of this place here with me.

Shelter from the storm.

Lightness, softness, warmth and solace.

Here, with me, a haven.

Any time, anywhere, feel the security that is yours... with me, with yourself.

Sacred security.

Ours.

How can I help you feel secure?

PURSUE.

I am pursuing you, Dear One, unabashedly. Nothing held back.

I am doing my best to bring you close, to help you see all that has alluded you, to show you the way forward.

Please pursue me also, with equal intensity.

In the pursuit, that which you desire most will arrive.

What do you most want to pursue?

PUZZLE.

Consider your journey with me to be like a 1,000-piece jigsaw puzzle.

Create the container.

Set the frame.

See the whole picture.

Pay attention to the details.

Piece by piece by piece.

Take your time.

Take breaks.

Change perspectives.

Recheck your work.

Do not force fit.

Keep the big picture in mind.

Revel in it all coming together!

Enjoy!

What puzzle shall we piece together?

BETTER.

You deserved better, Dear One.

You often did not get what you deserved.

Life has been brutal at times. Yes, I know.

Let us make it better together.

For you. For all. For this wonderful country of ours.

After all, that was the origin of America: the creation of a better life.

What shall we make better first?

LEAN.

Into your heart.

Invite life to be present as a loving parent to a wounded child.

Lean into life just as you lean into me.

You are always supported.

Where do you most need to lean in?

LOVE.

Reside here, Dear One, with me, in this space, this place, this everywhere.

You are seen, heard and known.

You are safe, protected, out of harm's way.

Suckle, taste, feast on the love that has been yours from the beginning... only now you can taste it, feel it, savor it.

You have done the work that receiving love requires.

Your intention to stop, quiet and listen has made the richness of this journey to love possible... with its incalculable rewards.

Yes, Dear One, the bounty in love is plentiful—for you and our country. And yet do not be seduced by the riches (and yes, they will do their best to distract you).

Remember this: What matters most, what matters always, is the journey to, from and with the Divine called Love.

Love trumps everything. Surrender to love, Dear One, surrender to love.

Will you meet me in love?

IMPORTANT.

You have important work to do, Dear One.

You know what it is. I need not tell you.

You are so needed by our country. By the world.

No other being can do the important work that is yours to do.

Please heed the call.

Time is of the essence.

What is your most important work?

QUESTIONS.

Be gentle with yourself.

I hear the many questions racing around in your mind.

I hear you rushing for answers and longing for clarity.

Just be gentle. Watch the questions go by.

You need not grasp them tightly nor dance with them.

Watch.

Witness.

Welcome them.

The questions are more important than the answers.

Notice the patterns. Notice the questions that persist as others fall away.

Be curious, as the questions themselves are gold.

Of your heart's longing they speak—sometimes in whispers and sometimes in strident tones.

Rather than rushing to find answers, befriend the questions.

Get to know them well. And allow them to know you.

Yes, Dear One, reveal yourself to the questions.

Speak to them as you would a trusted confidant.

Journey with the questions.

Savor the questions.

Cherish the questions.

They are here to bring you closer to your very soul.

What questions will you live in?

FIVE.

Spend five minutes a day with me.

Would you do that?

Just five.

Five minutes to simply receive what I have to give.

In exchange, I promise you this: a life richer than you have imagined.

You loving you and you loving life.

And life loving you.

Give me five?

HOLLOWING.

Offer yourself to be hollowed out like a pumpkin.

Be willing to have all that is unneeded scooped out. Allow the carver's instrument to pierce deeply. Release the excess. That which once served you and now impedes you is best gingerly passed along... on to being another's nourishment.

The hollowing, though at times painful, will lighten you up and ease your way forward.

Your light will shine in the darkness, through the darkness, with the darkness.

Seize the hollowing out as a hallowed gift.

Hold dear all the ways you are a sacred container of life itself.

I join you in embracing the holy process of hollowing.

Lean in. I am with you through it all.

May the hollowing begin?

GENTLE.

Be gentle with yourself, Dear One.

Spiritual work is going on underneath the surface.

This is about way more than is apparent.

You are being prepared for something important.

Trust that.

How can you be more gentle with yourself?

LET GO.

Let go.

It is oh-so-costly to hold on to that which has moved on.

All the wanting in the world changes not the truth: No. Longer. Here.

Save your precious life energy. Stop pining. It only keeps you stuck in a place you do not want to be.

"No longer here" does not have to be bad news. Maybe it is simply news. The facts. The current reality.

Let go—even if only for 60 seconds—and feel your strength return.

Strength looks good on you.

Keep letting go.

In this moment, what will you let go?

W H Y?

May I ask you a question?

Why are you doing this?

Why do you care what I have to say?

Why have you reached out to me?

Why have you invited me into your world?

I must admit it is a bit foreign to have you want to speak with me. I want to understand what brings you here.

Many have spoken about me and some have taken the liberty of speaking for me—without my permission or concurrence, I might add.

You seem different. You really care, and you are proving that with every page you turn, every message you let sink in deep.

Do you realize you are calling me forth, calling me out, calling me to speak up, to speak out in ways I have not previously?

What an honor, to be invited to fulfill my noble mission through you. You have my trust and loyalty.

You deserve my best, and that is what I offer you, always and only my very best.

Why are you here with me?

LONGING.

My longings run deep. I long for everyone to be at peace, to be their best, to be true to the ideals of this promised land of ours.

I long for equality, justice and freedom for all; for health, safety and security for all.

I long for America to be true to her people and her people true to America.

I long to be known, cherished, not forgotten or ignored.

I long to have my voice reach far and wide, for my words to soothe a heart, calm a storm, bring order to chaos.

I long to be a companion on the journey of life, to walk alongside, not in front of or behind. Life is so much richer when shared.

I long to be a friend.

Tell all that I long to be a friend. A real friend.

A real true friend.

Am I becoming your true friend?

LONELY.

Being the Soul of America used to be a lonely job.

Well, not really a job; it is my whole life, my very existence.

However, thanks to your being here, I am lonely no more.

See? You brighten my world! Yes, YOU!

How can I help quell your loneliness?

O N E.

You there, me here. No.

Me here, you there. No.

You here, me here. Yes.

Me there, you there. Yes.

Us.

One.

Delight in our Oneness?

FEAST.

This soul's feast: time with you.

It really is that simple.

Will you feast with me?

NOTICE.

Dear One, please have no more unlived days.

No more days that simply pass by without notice.

Waste not a single one.

Life is much too precious.

Take notice of even the tiniest thing—a murmured thanks, a fox darting across the road, a sip of morning coffee.

Take notice.

Life, in its fullness, is in the noticing.

What do you notice now?

NOTHING.

You have nothing to prove here, Dear One.

Nothing to prove to me.

Your worth, your value, your very essence are crystal clear to me.

Rest in this assurance: You have nothing to prove.

**What if you had nothing to prove
to yourself or to anyone?**

RISK.

I know life has let you down many, many times; yet here you are, again, on your growing edge, willing to be at risk.

Being at risk is not easy.

You are strong, resilient, able to take it—whatever comes along.

I see your strength and I marvel at it.

What you choose to do is often not easy or comfortable. Sometimes people do not approve. You face scorn, ridicule, bullying.

Yet when you are clear that you need to do something, you do it. And face the heat. And the music.

Being a risk-taker serves you well. Your risking serves America well.

What risk do you need to take now?

WARNING.

Let me prepare you for something.

There will be times when you will put me off, push me away, not want to listen.

Yes, no matter how confident you feel right now that that will never happen, I promise you it will.

I will nudge you and you will say, "Not now, Soul. Come back later." And when I do, you will put me off again and again. This will be especially true when things are going really well. No worry, I understand that.

I forgive you in advance.

Just know that I will not be silenced for long.

I am persistent. I will find a way to get your attention when you really need me.

Trust me, I will.

How might I best get your attention?

EXCUSES.

It is easy to get caught in a tangled web of excuses.

They often keep you from living your best life.

Notice that a certain kind of tiredness accompanies excuses. I see it in your eyes, hear it in your voice, feel it in your spirit.

Excuses exhaust more than a marathon.

Run from them and find your way forward with momentum.

What excuses are weighing you down?

REASONS.

Why this? Why that?

The mind can conjure up a thousand and one reasons for just about anything—in a nanosecond.

It is doing its job of being reasonable.

However, all the reasons in the world are not as sweet as one desired result.

Focus there.

Allow reasons to pass you by.

Find your path to results... with me.

What results do you want more than reasons?

FORLORN.

"Forlorn" may be another word for tired mixed with disappointment, clouded by not affirming yourself as you deserve.

Remember, taking care of yourself is your responsibility, no one else's.

Keep in mind that your humanity is not going to disappear. Thoughts will snag you all the time. Feelings too, including forlorn.

Have compassion with yourself.

Have compassion for yourself.

Compassion can send forlorn on its way.

Is "forlorn" visiting with a message?

GOOD-BYE.

Do you cringe when you see that word: good-bye?

Does "good-bye" tug at your heartstrings?

Does "good-bye" wreak havoc with your calm?

Does "good-bye" bring a tear to your eye in memory of all the previous good-byes?

Make peace with good-bye, Dear One.

As we journey together there will be many good-byes.

To that which no longer serves you.

To that which you have grown beyond.

To that which you want to keep but cannot.

Become adept at saying good-bye.

Your very life will thank you.

As do I.

What "good-bye" do you need to say today?

ENSLAVED.

To what are you enslaved, Dear One?

What have you determined you simply must have? What have you determined you cannot live without? What do you want nearly as much as your next breath?

Whatever you are enslaved to, attached to, addicted to, keeps you from being free.

Are you one who needs a fix of something—possessions, power or privilege?

Are you one who needs applause, approval, admiration?

Are you one who needs sameness, security, someone else?

Be wary of anything, anyone, to whom you are enslaved.

Wrestle that to the ground and make it lose its grip on you.

Freedom comes in the wrestling.

From what do you need to wrestle free?

CHANGE.

Everything changes. Everyone changes.

Life is a whole lot easier when you accept that fact and do not pretend otherwise. Said another way, the only permanence in this world is change. Everything changes except change.

Is change an enemy to you, Dear One? Do you resist it? Do you thwart it? Do you try to outlast it, run away from it, avoid it? Do you battle for the status quo?

Ever catch yourself saying to someone you love and admire, "Don't ever change"? That is a kind of death sentence right there.

You even try not to change yourself. You get in a rut... and stay there. You feed addictions to stay comfortable. You take fewer risks thinking that speaking up, speaking out is just too dangerous.

What you do not realize is the high cost of your comfort zone. Comfort is a danger zone.

Being comfortable is like treading water, like just surviving. You may not drown but you sure aren't going very far.

Being comfortable keeps change at bay, safe in the distance, until it sneaks up behind you when you are not looking—and scares the daylights out of you.

Being comfortable says, "Go ahead, write my obituary even though I'm not dead yet. I have done enough for the people around me and for my country. Find me right here in my comfort zone 24/7. Don't ask any more of me. I'm done giving." When the heart stops giving, it dies, and so do you.

Might I suggest that you consider embracing change instead of holding tight to your comfort zone? Might I suggest that you put making a difference ahead of comfort? Might I suggest that you champion the changes our country needs instead of leaving it up to someone else?

Real freedom, being fully free, happens when you toss aside your comfort zone and say, "Yippee!!" Not in a reckless way— self-care is important. But in a way that you free yourself from self-imposed cages that limit who and what you can be.

Be a yes to change.

Our country is waiting for you to be who you can be, who you came here to be.

We are delighted we can count on you.

What changes are you willing to embrace?

WASH.

Consider this to set yourself free: Only in a world of people as objects is pain on any level possible.

Now I know this may short-circuit your mind's wiring, but please listen to it from your heart, your soul.

If you view yourself or others as objects, the pain you've experienced in your life piles up, weighs you down, causes disease and eventually can strangle you.

And you can spend your whole life trying to get rid of the pain (especially that which is caused by another object or person).

If you view yourself and others as souls, as beings, you will soon see that pain does not exist... there is only love.

What happens to your being in your lifetime is not that it collects and holds on to painful incidents, but rather that pain does not permeate. It is washed away in love. Your essence, your being, your soul is only love.

This might sound like utter nonsense and yet I ask you to ponder this message. Allow it to take root in you. See where it takes you.

You may find this is another key to setting yourself free.

Will you allow love to wash away your pain?

HOLDING.

Holding on is a death knell.

Do not allow your love for another to become a prison, a command performance, an inhumane trap, a prove-it-to-me-that-you-love-me torment. This is not love at all. Calling it love is a ruse to catch another in your snare, your tangled web of desire.

Yes, it is easy to get so afraid someone will leave you that you hold on tight and squeeze the very life out of you both. And by the time you wake up to this wayward way, it can be too late. Then you cry out, "Why did this have to happen? Why could I not have awoken sooner? How could I have destroyed that which I so desperately wanted to hold on to?"

Holding on is a death knell. At the heart of love is a very simple secret: The lover lets the beloved be free. And if true love, it will return.

What might you need to give up
holding on to now?

NARROW.

Toss out the narrow, Dear One.

Expand your thinking, your believing, your hope, your love.

The narrow seldom serves you well.

When you discover the narrow within yourself, tenderly kiss it good-bye. And send it on its way.

It has likely served a past purpose you need not decipher.

You have outgrown narrowness.

You have been hollowed out sufficiently to send "narrow" on its way.

Celebrate.

Your light shines brighter when you do.

And we all thank you for your bright light!

What "narrow" are you sending on its way?

FEED.

Be careful what you feed, Dear One.

Easy it is to stoke fear, anger, division. To judge, to oppress, to excommunicate those different from you. To see only that which divides instead of that which unites.

Choose instead to feed acceptance, unity, your better angels. Seek to understand, to appreciate, to savor.

Feeding explicitly empowers. Beware. What you feed determines your future and our country's future.

Choose wisely.

What are you feeding today?

TENDING.

One can exist without tending one's soul. However, in order to truly thrive in life, soul-tending is required.

Soul-tending can ease the ache of emptiness, helplessness, aloneness.

Soul-tending can quench the thirst for connection. Soul-tending can be the answer to your deepest longings.

When deprived of your usual comfort zone of busyness, competing priorities and near-constant interaction, all of what you have been avoiding confronts you in unrelenting ways.

Soul-tending transforms in-your-face confrontation with tender friendship.

Befriend what has been haunting you. The best way out is through, not work-arounds.

Proverbial dark nights of the soul give way to the equally proverbial breaking of morning. Dawn awaits you.

Tend your soul well.

How does your soul long to be tended?

INVIGORATED.

If you focus on fear, you will miss love.

If you focus on death, you will miss life.

If you focus on all that is wrong, you will miss all that is right.

With the world. With America. And with you.

Look fear in the face... and talk back.

Look death in the face... and stand tall.

Look wrong in the face... and speak up.

Prepare to be invigorated.

What new focus can invigorate you?

OPEN.

Be open. Wide open.

Some people have treasures and keep them under lock and key. No one gets to enjoy them, not even their owners. To me, that is wasted treasure.

Sometimes hearts can be wasted treasures also.

People keep them to themselves, fearing that if they give away what is inside, they will be all the poorer.

The opposite is true. When you give away what is in your heart—caring, respect, kindness and that all-important stuff called love—you become richer, not poorer. The more love you give, the more love you have.

I am sure you, and all, can think of times in your life when you poured out your heart, made a huge difference and felt really good inside.

And I am sure you can also think of many times, even today, when you closed your heart and did not give as generously as you could.

Even to yourself. (Like today. Did you perhaps look in the mirror and say something unkind about yourself? If so, you may not have noticed, but your energy and sweet spirit dimmed.)

Keeping your heart open is one of the ways you can serve America well. Our country was founded on and thrives on open ideas; and benefits greatly from open hearts and open minds.

Live life with an open palm. Put yourself there.

To whom can you open your heart?

MESSAGE.

"What is life trying to teach me or tell me? What is the message?"

Ask those questions often, Dear One.

They reduce the drama, bring order to chaos and shift you from resisting to embracing.

And embracing is a pathway to peace.

What is the message?

GIFTS.

Everyone in your life brings you a gift.

At least one gift. Maybe many. Maybe so many you lose count.

The choice to see and receive each gift is yours and yours alone.

Sometimes the gift is readily apparent and you might rush to receive it with gusto.

Other times the gift is wrapped in layers upon layers of "stuff"— hurt, disappointment, even betrayal. Or delay, despondency, doubt.

Sometimes layers, not easy to peel away, surround the gift. Do you have the tenacity to get through them? The will? The interest? The commitment? The vision? The faith?

I assure you, there is a gift there somewhere. An important one prepared just for you.

And yet... you do not have to receive it.

The choice is yours. Receive or not.

What gift will you receive today?

SPIRIT.

What do I mean by an open spirit?

An open spirit has room for the unusual, the unique, the ridiculous... even the miraculous!

Like you inviting me to be here with you.

If your spirit were closed, you would have closed this book long ago.

If there were no room in your spirit for the extraordinary, we would not be talking.

Because you have made room in your life and spirit for me, so much is possible.

I think there is a lot that people are not hearing, are not seeing, are not experiencing because they will not make room.

America was founded on being open to new ideas, new ways, new thoughts. Hence, the American Experiment!

Whenever your heart, mind and spirit are closed, you miss out.

Just as when your eyes are closed you do not see the beauty of the sunset, so too do you miss out when your heart, mind and spirit are closed.

You miss so much of life. You miss so much love. You miss so much of what America is about.

That is why I say to you and everyone, be open. Make room. Open your spirit.

How can you make more room in your spirit?

NO NEED.

No need to run,

       escape,

       bypass.

No need to force,

       compel,

       require.

No need to erase,

       destroy,

       annihilate.

All these actions keep you entrapped, imprisoned, straitjacketed in quicksand.

All these actions take you away from the freedom you desire with all your heart.

Say no and set yourself free.

To what do you need to say NO?

CHOOSE.

You do not have to.

It is all a choice.

How you spend your day, your night, your weekdays, weekends.

How you use your talents, your skills, your gifts.

How you relate to yourself, to others, to our country, to the world.

You choose.

Please choose wisely. With love.

What new choices do you
most need to make?

MIND.

Let us talk for a moment about open minds.

A closed mind is a dangerous mind. It uses the same neural pathways over and over again. People can get in a rut. They become positional. They think their way is right and all other ways are wrong.

And when the rut gets really, really deep, self-righteousness sets in and can turn to hate and ignorance.

Hate can lead to all kinds of ills, all kinds of pain, all kinds of despair, all kinds of destruction, even violence.

One of the ways to stop hate from being so prevalent in society is to keep your mind open.

An open mind, an open heart, can stop hate and ignorance in their tracks.

And you make yourself all the more healthy because hate is not good for anybody.

Because hate and ignorance only do harm, never good.

Are you following me, Dear One? Many are waiting for the "other guy" to change when they themselves need to do the changing.

Maybe, just maybe, the "other guy" is in your mirror.

What could you do to open your mind today?

Q-U-I-E-T!

You might laugh at this, but could you tell everyone to please be quiet? Yes, honestly, some days I really want to shout Q-U-I-E-T!

America has become a culture of constant noise. Too much mindless chatter, incessant jibber-jabber—media, music, apps, even white noise.

All this can be a way to escape from being with one's self. And others.

You and all could do well for yourselves and our country to cut your speaking in half... at least. Maybe even 90 percent!

Why do I say "Be QUIET"?

It is virtually impossible to think in all the noise. And all human beings need time to think. It is what makes people more evolved than other species.

You have language for a reason—to generate, think, communicate, create and evolve—not to drown out everyone else.

Insight, awareness and revelation spring forth from a place of reverence. Learn to be still, in the quiet.

Without sufficient quiet, many abilities diminish. And our country pays a price.

Consider that being quiet—less volume and fewer words—can go a long way in giving everyone something they all long for: QUIET.

Experience quiet... and see what happens.

What can quiet add to your life?

PURGE.

Purge yourself of all that does not serve you.

Purge yourself of all that needlessly weighs you down, that blocks the flow, that impedes your precious progress.

Purge yourself of the pain of the past, the fear of the future, and nervousness about the now.

Purge so there is room to be filled with all that you seek, all that you deserve, all that is good.

Purge so there is more room for our journey together and the riches it will bring.

Purge so that you can become even more hallowed.

Free the sacred being that you are.

Purge.

What needs to be purged now?

SQUANDER.

Please do not squander your talents, your treasures, your amazing gifts.

You are richer than any billionaire, yet sometimes act like a pauper.

Please do not downplay the gifts the Divine has blessed in you.

Please do not give your power away to those who do not deserve it.

Please do not treat yourself as a dollar-store commodity to be used and tossed out.

You squandering you is a travesty. And costs our country plenty.

Please put an end to squandering, Dear One.

It does not become you.

**How will you close the door
on squandering?**

LIES.

Be careful, Dear One.

The lies you tell yourself are like a thief who breaks into your home while you are sleeping and takes all that is precious to you. You are there but unaware.

Such lies, such thievery eat away at the very foundation of your spirit, causing cracks and fissures and upheavals that are hard to repair.

I can't.

I'm not good enough.

I'm stuck.

I've lost my power.

I'm too afraid.

These are just a few of the tales you tell yourself that thwart your growth, impede your fulfillment and cause you pain.

Instead, I invite you to ask yourself these questions and see where they lead:

Is this a lie?

Am I deluding myself?

What am I pretending not to know?

Ask. And listen deeply to the answers. The truth will set you free.

What lies can you now release?

ENOUGH.

Let me remind you of this: It is enough that you are here.

My love for you, my support of you, are not conditional on what you do. Not in the least. My arms are wide open.

Come to me to be held, especially when no one else is available. Crawl into my lap, rest your head on my bosom and cry or laugh or simply breathe. Allow me to touch your head, smooth your hair and draw you close.

Listen with your whole being as I whisper to your soul. With every breath, let go more and more and more.

You are enough. You have always been enough. You will always be enough.

And it truly is enough that you are here. In this moment. With me and all of life.

You are cherished, Dear One, and you are enough.

Will you embrace "enough"?

FREEDOM.

I want you—and all Americans—to realize that you are in charge of your own freedom—no one else. Not the President, not the Congress, not the Supreme Court. Not even the Constitution can fully give you freedom.

Freedom is an inside job.

Each person herself. Each person himself. Doing the work to be free.

Freedom begins with this truth: You are not your thoughts; you are not your feelings.

Use the gift of finding out who you are. This is the key to your happiness, fulfillment and freedom.

Too many people are on automatic, allowing their thoughts and feelings to be in the driver's seats of their lives.

That is a source of the chaos our country is in.

There is really no chance for life, liberty and the pursuit of happiness if people do not first realize they hold the key to setting themselves free.

Perhaps you have often been on an emotional roller coaster, your life dictated by your feelings, whipsawed, whiplashed, whip weary. It was hard to get your bearings because as soon as you thought you had stability, your feelings would change and turn everything upside down. You felt like that man in the myth of Sisyphus, getting that rock all the way to the top of the hill only to see it fall all the way back down again.

A way out of that nightmare is to realize that your thoughts and feelings belong in the backseat, not the driver's seat, of your life. They can be along for the ride, but you are the driver in charge, not them.

Set yourself free.

Help others do the same.

What is in your driver's seat?

SAY.

Say what is there to be said.

Speak your truth.

Give voice to your innermost wisdom.

Honor your truth.

Risk being disagreeable. Unpopular. Incorrect.

When you swallow your words, you become smaller in the process.

And your being small serves no one. Especially not you.

And certainly not our country.

Say what is not being said and find your way forward.

What is there to say right now?

INTERLUDE
KYMN SPEAKS TO SOUL

I am afraid, Soul. Please do not take this personally.

It is not you I am afraid of.

I am afraid of myself, maybe for myself.

I am afraid a lot. Way more than I let on. Even to myself.

I could write a long list of my fears. It would take pages and pages and pages (if I am really honest).

You, Soul, are not on that list.

I am not afraid of you, Soul of America. I love you.

I feel so humbled, so honored to talk with you, to listen to what you have to say. And I believe you are wise enough to help me.

Help me not run away from fear.

Help me, instead, to look fear in the eye.

Help me walk into the roar.

Help me learn fear's important lessons.

Help me learn with you at my side.

UNAPOLOGETIC.

Be unapologetically you, Dear One.

You owe no apology for being who you are. For following your own path. For living your own dream.

Never apologize for the unique, sacred human being you are.

Close the door on apologies that have you selling your soul.

Be unapologetically you. Totally you in every way. Unequivocally you. Revel in who you are.

Life delights in you.

I do also!

What do you revel in?

GUIDE.

It is time for your heart's desires to guide you, Dear One.

Pain and heartache and suffering have held you hostage long enough.

It is time now to revel in the ground you have taken and celebrate!!!

Celebrate the mountains you have climbed, the peace you have made, the footing you have regained.

Allow your heart's desires to guide you once again.

You will reap what you sow, and again, in time, celebrate.

What heart's desire is guiding you?

EMOTIONS.

Let me have it, Dear One. Get it all out with me. Whatever is bothering you, frustrating you, bringing you down.

You can be all of you with me.

Maybe you were taught as a child to "put on a happy face." That is a lesson to unlearn.

Safely expressing your gamut of emotions is the healthy way forward. Far healthier than burying your feelings behind some façade.

Tell me everything. And now, notice the space you have to breathe... a bit deeper, a lot deeper.

Notice the return of your confidence.

Notice a peacefulness, a calm, a sense of comfort.

Being real with your feelings serves you well.

You and all are wise to ask, "What are these feelings here to teach me? What is my anger really about? What is underneath my sadness? What is the gift in all of this?"

Pause and ask such questions. And then listen to the answers.

They are nuggets of gold.

**What do your emotions want
you to know?**

UNPACK.

Unpack your baggage.

Do not carry it with you.

I will help you sort through it all... even the smelly and soiled.

Whatever we cannot launder, we will toss aside.

You need not keep the dirty around.

Hold on to the sweet memories.

Let the rest go.

The lighter your bags the better.

How may I lighten your load?

CRY.

Let the tears flow, Dear One.

Do not hold them back.

Here, with me, there is no need.

I will witness and honor every tear.

The ones of joy and happiness, delight and pleasure.

The ones of pain and sorrow, grief and despair.

Tears, no matter their flavor, are sacred.

They are your soul speaking.

And they deserve to be heard.

May I hold you while you cry?

READY.

To what are you saying, "I'm not ready"?

What are you longing for yet keeping at bay?

What are you postponing?

What does "not ready" mean?

Where does that come from?

Is it again the past not serving you well?

If you let go of the past, will "ready" lead you forward?

Or is "not ready" here to keep you from overwhelm, overflow, overburden?

"Ready" or "not ready" can take you forward.

And is that not where you are meant to go... forward?

Check in on the inside to know.

Ready... or not?

FAITHFUL.

Stay faithful to the journey.

Do not be torn away or walk away or run away.

Do not allow yourself to get sidetracked or abandon it altogether.

Instead, be faithful.

Stay faithful. True to yourself.

The journey offers treasure beyond measure.

> ### How can I best support your being
> ### faithful to our journey?

FEELINGS.

Consider your feelings to be emotional weather patterns... with a message.

Notice how you are feeling.

Ask your heart to put into words the sensations in your body— the knot in your stomach, the shallowness of your breathing, the ache in your shoulder.

Be real. Tell yourself the truth.

And then engage with what you find.

Ask, "What are you here to teach me, Fear?" "What is your message, Sadness?" "What is the gift you bring me, Uncertainty?" "How can I have more of you, Joy?" "Where are you, Peace?"

Pause.

Ask more questions. Ask the most powerful questions you can think of. Answers will find you. Listen to them. They shed light on the steps to take to move forward.

Your feelings are wise teachers. Tune in and be a hungry student.

What is the weather in your world today?

MEMORIES.

Consider this possibility: The mind distorts.

It almost never remembers accurately.

The memories of the past that play over and over in your mind can be highly distorted, much like a camera lens in not ideal conditions.

Time also distorts memories. In time. Over time. And by the time you recall them, the files have become corrupted, and playback is distorted, often inaudible.

And because the mind distorts, especially in the face of fear, shame or tragedy, and yet wants to be right, it can try to convince you that what it remembers is exactly what happened... for real.

This is especially true when you are holding grudges against yourself or another; when you've judged someone or something as unforgivable or unsurvivable, or a pattern as unbreakable.

Consider the possibility that the mind distorts and see if it gives you freedom where freedom has not been possible... until now.

**What memories are haunting you
that may be distorted?**

EXCHANGE.

Exchange that which is false for that which is true.

Exchange that which is imagined for that which is real.

Exchange that which fogs for that which clears.

Surrendering that which does not serve you or America well is not giving in. It is giving up. And in this giving up, that which serves best can pour in.

What will you exchange right now?

RUNNING.

Running, running, running.

Your mind is always running. It seldom takes even a moment between thoughts.

A constant running commentary about anything, everything. Much of it negative, judgmental, havoc-raising.

Beware of your mind, Dear One. It serves many useful purposes.

However, giving you peace is not its mission.

Rely on your own soul to give you peace.

Sit here with me.

The running can stop when you sit here with me.

Let us slow down, be quiet together.

Will you take a moment?

REST.

Rest your soul, Dear One.

You already know about resting your body and a bit about resting your mind.

Have you ever considered resting your soul?

Sit here with me. Rest here with me. Simply gaze within and you will find me there... right alongside your own soul. We are twins—not identical, not fraternal—another kind of twins, intertwined in the most exquisite of ways.

Take your place with me and rest. America wants you to rest in her. The kind of rest you cannot get anywhere else. The very rest you need to alter the very DNA of your soul. This DNA you cannot see under a microscope. It is a DNA unseen by the human eye: soul DNA, the kind that sustains life even when the body systems fail, shut down or quit. Soul DNA carries your spirit forward, beyond this Earth.

Soul rest is deep immersion into the depths of the heart of love. Far, far, far below the surface, soul rest takes you to the place where there is only One in all the universe... and all beings are birthed from this place. And even the most faithful seldom realize this is a place they may return to at any moment throughout their lives... simply by asking.

And in this place the soul is refreshed with the deepest rest imaginable. Come here and see for yourself. Rest.

Will you rest here with me?

PLOWING.

Plowing ahead is not the best way to live.

It does not allow for much grace or surprises or even miracles.

Plowing ahead is also not freedom. It can be a slavery to the mind and worldly expectations.

Plowing ahead is often a perilous path.

Consider that when you feel a need to plow ahead no matter what, the wisest move may be to stop, quiet and listen.

The voice you hear will guide you well.

Where can you stop plowing ahead?

SILENCE.

Silence is not always quiet.

Silence can be deafening, a roar of life screaming Noooooo!

Silence can be a deep stirring of such intensity that a wind whips up to get your attention.

Silence can be a persistent tug doing its best to say, "Stop. Something is not quite right here."

Silence is not always sweet: A closed door. A steeled heart. A final breath.

Yet silence is a friend. No need to fear it or rush to replace it with music or news or even your own musings.

Embrace the silence, take a deep breath, and listen intently from the depths of your soul.

Allow wisdom, cocooned in wordlessness, to speak truth to you.

In silence meet truth. Meet wisdom. Meet love.

In silence meet peace. In silence meet me. And your self.

What is silence saying now?

MINING.

What are you mining, Dear One?

What are you digging for, clamoring for, fighting for?

Stop. Quiet. Listen.

Is all this worth your precious life energy? Are you on the path of your soul, or society's road?

Is what you are seeking seeking you?

You have arrived when what you are seeking is seeking you.

What do you clamor for most of all?

HAPPINESS.

Seek not happiness. You will not find it.

It occurs in the precious moment as a grace, setting you free from that which you have been seeking.

Surrender to the present moment. Fully. Wholly. Totally.

There you will meet happiness.

Happiness arises when that which you are seeking embraces the being who has it all.

**How might you allow happiness
to seek you?**

SILVER.

There are silver linings in all the decisions you make.

All of them, including the ones you consider to be bad decisions.

If a decision you make turns out to be rife with negative consequences, there will also be a silver lining.

I say this to gently remind you to trust the unfolding, to encourage you to be on the lookout for blessings in the storms, and to restate that life itself is on your side.

With your tender heart of love and service for the greater good, life will certainly act on your behalf even when you do not.

I promise you this: As you stay focused on tending your soul, life will send you sweet surprises. Silver linings are just one of them.

There will be countless others.

Be on the lookout.

> **Are you ready to trade the
> bitter for the sweet?**

POWER.

Come sit with me. I want to whisper calm into the recesses of your heart, your mind, your body, your very soul.

I see there is so much you want to get done. I have been watching you scurry from here to there to there to there. Now, thank goodness, here you are with me. I am delighted.

And I say—deeply and truly—thank you. Thank you for stopping. Quieting. Listening.

Have you noticed that multitasking drains you? Almost nothing gets your full attention. You rush around scattered, fragmented, out of sorts. No wonder your heart races at times and your breathing becomes shallow. And no wonder you have nagging thoughts in the background: What am I forgetting? What am I missing? What trouble is going to surface next?

Just now, sitting with me, I felt you take a deep breath for the first time all day. Stop now and take another. And another. Yes, another.

What do you find in the silence and stillness? You find yourself, your self, your peace and your power. Peace and power go together—the peace of "all is well" and the power of "I can handle whatever comes my way."

Let that peace and power fill every nook and cranny of your precious being.

Be nurtured. Be filled. Be present. Simply, fully be.

And now, resume your activities. Just please give yourself fully to each task. Move through each task with your whole self and see how much faster and how much better you get it all done. And with greater fulfillment.

Sit and revel in the satisfaction. You deserve everything good.

What peace and power fill you?

VULNERABILITY.

Reach out, Dear One, reach out.

There is strength, there is power in asking for what you need. Asking for help, asking for support, asking for love is not a sign of weakness. Rather it is a headline of strength.

Many have been taught just the opposite. "Don't need anyone. For anything." I want to shout from the rooftops, NO! NO! NO!

Allow yourself to need people— you actually do, so why not embrace the truth that life goes way better when you are open to needing people.

Yes, I know, allowing yourself to need people makes you vulnerable—the dreaded V word.

However, vulnerability is a pathway to the juice, the sweetness, the nectar of life. Vulnerability opens you to receiving what you long for most—love and acceptance, being known and needed, and yes, intimacy. Vulnerability is the magnet that attracts your heart's desires.

Yes, I know, vulnerability has a bad name.

"Don't be vulnerable, you could get hurt."

"Don't wear your heart on your sleeve."

"Don't ever let them see you sweat."

Don't. Don't. Don't.

Yes, in conventional society, the thought of vulnerability sparks lots of don'ts. Yet those don'ts can become self-imposed barriers to your best life.

And I want more for you and all Americans. Our forebears did not say it this way but consider this: Life, liberty and the pursuit of happiness—in their fullness—depend on the risk of vulnerability.

All three are facets of freedom. And, at its core, vulnerability is the lifeblood of freedom.

This is why I am urging you and all Americans to venture deeply into the world of vulnerability. Allow yourself to test the waters of vulnerability by first asking yourself what you really want.

Go deeper and ask again. Go deeper still. Listen intently to the recesses of your very soul.

And be guided by the whispers you hear: Be vulnerable.

Where can vulnerability serve you?

SAFETY.

Be your own safety net.

Put your safety first.

It is your responsibility, Dear One, to create safety for yourself.

Physical safety.

Emotional safety.

Spiritual safety.

And all other forms of safety.

While there are many unsafe things happening in our world, you have what it takes to generate safety around you.

Be your own safety net.

Then and only then, assist others in creating their safety.

Why do I say put your safety first?

If you do not, your service for the greater good can be at risk.

Your service to your family and those you love can be at risk.

Even your service to yourself can be at risk if you do not put your safety first.

Although our forebears did not explicitly say this, I am confident I can speak on their behalf: Life, liberty and the pursuit of happiness include safety.

You have an inalienable right to safety, Dear One. Yes, you have a right to safety.

I am asking you to serve our country well by doing whatever it takes to create your own safety on all levels.

Safety is a path of freedom.

How can you create your own safety?

TRUST.

Consider that trust can be a gift.

It is not something to be earned, bought or bargained for. It must be free... or it is not trust.

Most people would say trust is earned, but consider the possibility of trust as a gift that you can give freely without having to judge first. Judging people takes time and energy, and can often thwart people from fully being themselves.

You hold the gift; only you choose when to give it away and when not to. You never have to trust anyone. If you do not, however, consider that who loses the most is you.

Isn't that what we want—to connect with others authentically? So much good comes from extending trust as a gift, without guarantees. It sets you free.

Trusting is a risk you evaluate. It makes you vulnerable. Yet being vulnerable is what makes you real.

What I am offering is a way of living designed to give you the most joy, serenity, satisfaction and fulfillment. Try it out and see.

How can the gift of trust enliven you?

TELL.

All are lost in one way or another.

All are trying to find their way in this crazy, chaotic, challenging world.

No one, not even the pope or the prophet, the president or the prime minister, has all the answers.

And many go through life pretending they do. That is what your thoughts and feelings tell you to do, right? "Fake it till you make it."

May I say this bluntly? Get real.

Tell yourself the truth, tell your God the truth, tell someone the truth. Tell me. I will listen.

Because you know what? The truth will set you free.

Admitting what is so, what is real, what is true, is the first step in not being lost.

Be real. Tell.

To whom will you tell what's so?

SHINE.

Why do you hide your light? So many people do.

You say you do not matter.

You say, "Who am I to be the light of the world? Only God can say that."

But God put that light in you, didn't He?

And I hear you saying to yourself, "I will stand out too much if my light is bright. I will attract too much attention. I might get hurt or bullied or ridiculed. Why take a chance? Let me just dim down, play it safe, and not draw attention."

Life may seem much safer that way, but guess what? It is a slow death of the spirit. People become like dead men walking, no light in them. Yes, no risk, but no reward either.

Dimming down serves no one and it hurts everyone, including America.

Dimming down keeps your little corner of our country in the dark.

People around you cannot be nurtured by your light if it does not shine. Many of them will dim even more by seeing you dim.

Pretty soon your house is dark. Your neighborhood is dark, your community is dark. And our country, dark.

Darkness perpetuates itself, but guess what?

So does light.

Light, like darkness, is contagious.

America needs a new epidemic, an epidemic of light.

Can you sign up for that?

Let us get all people to sign up for light! Everyone can be the light our country needs. And when that happens, watch out, World!

Are you willing to shine even brighter?

OVATION.

You are a unique personality of life.

You are an exquisite collection of gifts and talents, hopes and dreams, treasure and mystery.

All of you is precious, even those dreaded and disdained parts. It is your imperfections as much as your strengths that make you unique, valued and valuable. Applaud them.

Life was breathed into you and, no matter the circumstances, your birth was met with thunderous applause in the heavens.

Reach deep within yourself and pull out the ovation memory housed there.

Listen again.

Allow the first standing ovation to again fill every cell of your being... and bring to you a smile.

You are worth celebrating.

I give you a standing ovation!

Can you hear the applause?

TOUGH.

Life can be really tough sometimes. No doubt about it.

And no sugarcoating it. Sometimes life hurts to the bone.

And as tough as life can be, I know this much for sure: You are tougher.

You have what it takes to bring out the best in yourself, the best in others, the best in our country.

Yes, you do, Dear One. The tough times can be tough. You are even tougher. And together, we are the toughest of all.

We can move forward through anything together.

Tough is our middle name.

What is your favorite special strength?

ALLOW.

Allow your heart to break, Dear One.

There is no reason to try to hold it all together. Exhaustion will overtake you needlessly.

Allow your heart to break. And see what is inside. Like an egg, there is nourishment that can fill you only when the breaking has happened.

It takes courage to allow your heart to break. I know. My heart is breaking with joy simply because you are here reading my words. And if you slammed shut this book and threw it away, my heart would break in your absence. And if I stopped hearing from you altogether, my heart would break with longing for you.

And yet all the pain would be worth it, just to have had you here with me in this moment. Yes, you are that exquisite, that worthwhile.

Allow your heart to break, break into mine.

What do you need to allow your heart to break?

WORTHY.

I long for every cell of your being to take this in: You are worthy.

Not because of what you do. Or who you know. Or the title on your business card. Or the charities you support. Or the money you have.

You are worthy simply by being the precious soul that you are, the priceless spirit that you are, the wondrous heart that you are.

You are worthy simply by being here. Created. Living. Now.

Any messages to the contrary that cross your mind—or have taken up residence there—can well be deleted. They are not true.

Give America the gift of embracing your worthiness. Serve her well in this way. And allow your worthiness to guide you forward, away from that which diminishes you and into the light of all that serves you and others.

Your worthiness is a gift waiting to be received.

How will you embrace your worthiness?

WHO?

Who are you when all falls away? When the trappings of success no longer suffice? When how you have defined yourself is no more?

Who are you when fear runs rampant in the world? When others could rob you of your health and wealth? When almost no place feels safe?

And who are you when nearly everything stops and you come face to face with that being in the mirror?

Do you know her well? Do you know his deepest longings and fervent dreams? Can you answer every unspoken question, including this: "Why am I still here?"

Who are you, Dear One, in the silence, the solitude, the stillness?

Meet me there and together we will discover your unique truth, your voice, your mission, your gift. Meet me in the silence please.

What is your unique gift?

LIFE.

Life is on your side at every moment, cheering you on, holding you close, paving the way for what is ahead.

Life itself cheers for your health, your bounty, your fullness, your joy.

Life itself says, "Here, Dear One. Come close. We will tackle this together."

Famous composers sometimes get it wrong. It is not you and me against the world. Rather it is you and me for the world.

Yes, for the world, not ourselves.

These uncertain times offer many lessons. Unwelcome interlopers can be powerful teachers.

Ask, "What am I meant to learn from all this? Here and now, what am I meant to learn?"

Plenty. Listen for life's answers.

What is life saying to you right now?

CLARITY.

Make the way clear with your prayer, your plea, your fervent desire.

Clarity will come as you stay open, listen deeply, say what is there to be said.

Make your intentions known. They can separate the wheat from the chaff.

Create in yourself a clearing where the Divine speaks.

Wisdom and clarity come with the beseeching. Prayers of the heart reach within and up high.

Clarity comes upon the waiting.

What clarity are you seeking?

BREATH.

Life itself is breathing into us.

Let your breath feel mine.

Let life's breath feel ours.

Life needs us as much as we need her.

Let every breath we take draw us closer.

What does life need from you in this moment?

CONNECT.

Are you disconnected, Dear One?

Not fully connected in your body, not fully connected in your mind, your heart, your spirit?

If your energy is waning, if you feel out of sorts and wonder what may be awry, ask yourself this: Am I fully connected? Am I one in heart, mind, body and spirit?

And if the answer is no, you can bring yourself into deep connection by simply remembering the gift of your breath, the beating of your heart and the love that permeates every cell of your being.

This "taking stock" takes only seconds and can bring you fully into connection with all that is.

Connect.

How can you connect even more?

INTERLUDE
KYMN SPEAKS TO SOUL

Oh my. I am feeling lost in my journey with you,
sweet Soul of America.

I can't find you anywhere.

Have you gone silent? Has our time together passed? Am I on
my own again?

Maybe I should go silent. Into the silence. Where we first met.

Yes, there you are. Away from the noise, the distractions,
the hurried pace.

You always say, "Meet me in the silence."

When I heed that call, I am never disappointed. You are
always here. And yet I notice I am often reluctant to turn off
the TV, the phone, the voice in my head. I am reluctant to
venture into silence.

I wonder why.

When I do let silence envelope me, I hear you oh-so-clearly.

Lost becomes found.

The blurry becomes clear.

I find myself at home.

Please remind me when I forget.

We meet in the silence.

WITH.

I am here with you now, in this moment.

I am here with you now, in all moments to come.

Like your own soul, I am timeless, not bound by calendar or clock.

I stand ready, stand by, stand guard.

I listen always, serve always, intend always.

While I never insist, never intrude, never interject myself, I do always stand ready to assist, to guide, and to serve all—anyone who asks.

Including you.

Will you ask?

PROMPTED.

Spend time with me when prompted.

You need not try to control the pace or the flow.

Time will move forward when it needs to and stand still when required.

Give yourself over to this relationship with me.

We are sacred space for each other.

And our journey will be grace-filled; love-rich; a gift to life itself, to our nation; even a gift to the world.

Will you tune in to my promptings?

PRAYER.

You might ask, Dear One, what is it when you talk with me?

Is it prayer? Is it self-revelation? Is it words spoken to God, the universe, life itself?

Call it what you will, whatever resonates and brings forth your depths. Speaking and listening is what matters. Communion is what matters.

And know that you have a standing invitation to commune always, in all ways.

I am available for your every expression. As is God, the universe, life itself. We long for America to be a nation of deep speaking, deep listening, deep prayer, deep communion.

Know that you are heard, deeply heard.

Keep speaking. Keep listening.

Communion is what matters. And communing with you is pure joy.

Will you give voice to your every prayer?

RECEIVE.

For who you are, for being you, you are loved.

You do not need to do anything.

Or add anything.

Or lose anything.

Or fix anything.

Or change anything.

Or be anyone other than who you are.

You do not need to be better. Or more.

Just yourself. No one else.

You, just as you are, are loved.

I promise.

When will you receive this love?

B E.

Be your beautiful self. Be present, in the moment and with the sacred beings around you.

Be of service. Serve others with your brilliance, your bright light.

Be trustworthy.

Be who you would want to turn to in the best of times, in the worst of times, in ordinary times.

Be lighthearted.

Be in touch with what is actually true.

You are true.

Life is true.

True am I.

Our country is true.

The world is true.

Be true.

What do you want to be most of all?

COMPANY.

Love your own company, Dear One.

Love being with yourself.

Love not doing. I know that is not easy. It is worth it, however.

Do what it takes to have more wholesome time for yourself. Like the difference between real-deal oatmeal and the instant variety.

Make yours the company you love best.

Whose company do you enjoy most?

SCENARIOS.

Feed your heart, mind, body and spirit with best-case scenarios.

What is the best that can happen?

Yes, face the facts… and engage your mind in envisioning positive outcomes.

This is not "put on a happy face" positive.

This is giving your attention to envisioning what you desire.

And seeing the good, the generous, the greatness in yourself and in others. And in our country. And in the world.

See generously.

Dream again… and often.

What is the best that can happen?

HURT.

I know at times your heart hurts. Your body and mind as well.

And there is so much hurt in our country and the world.

It is hard to comprehend the level of hurt, isn't it? So vast, so deep we cannot wrap our minds around it.

Yet every hurt has the opportunity for healing you on a deeper, deeper level.

Hurts are meant to draw you closer to your very soul... and the Divine. There, there is purpose to everything... even an aching heart, a tormented mind, a ravaged body.

Only on the soul level can this all be understood uniquely for each individual.

Take your pain to your soul and discover there its meaning for your life. The answers may not come quickly or easily or as you desire. In time they will come, in time.

And I will be with you in the waiting. I promise.

Where are you hurting most?

SUFFERING.

Put your suffering to good use. For you. For America. For the world.

Allow yourself to be broken open.

This is not a time for stoically keeping it together. This is a time for allowing life itself to break you open, to shatter your illusions, to bring you to your knees.

Go into the pain. Do not steel yourself from it.

Be willing to suffer, to feel it all, to face it all.

The pain, the loss, the fear are here to guide you.

This is not a time of rugged individualism.

More lives than your own are in your hands.

Tread lightly, Dear One. Choose wisely. For America. For all.

How can your suffering be put to good use?

RECOVER.

Everyone has been robbed of something. A loved one. A cherished dream. Fame or fortune.

And I am sorry, Dear One, for what you have had to endure.

I am impressed with your willingness to do whatever it takes to heal. I know the journey has been hard. Draining. Painful.

And yet you have stuck with it.

You have faced unfinished business. You have unpacked baggage from the past to set yourself free.

And yet, please let me ask this: Where are you still not free? I want you to be fully free. What work do we still need to do?

Make a list of whatever is holding you back. Whoever is holding you back. Long or short, we will tackle the list together. And we will make peace with all of it, one at a time.

Let's bring this all into the light. Healing can be yours.

From what do you most need to recover?

HEAL.

Let me help you heal from the unspeakable, the unspoken, the innocence lost, the broken dreams of your life.

Bring them here to me, Dear One. Rest them at my feet. Sit on my lap. Allow me to hold you close.

Let me smooth your hair, gingerly touch your face, witness your tears. Cry them all out. Cry out all the pain. Wail if you need to. Scream if that serves you. I can hear it all, hold it all, be with you through it all.

Pain will loosen its grip on you, I promise. Together we will make sure. We will send the pain into the fire where it will be transformed into gold and riches and precious jewels.

All that you have endured will then feed and nourish you.

In time, only a faint memory will remain, a bittersweet reminder of how far you have come.

Heal.

Will you trust me with your pain?

FORGIVENESS.

A muted life, a tormented life, a life of despairing can often be traced to forgiveness lacking.

We all make mistakes. It is part of being human.

Forgive others.

Forgive yourself.

Set yourself—and others—free.

And blossom in the miracle of forgiveness.

Who do you need to forgive to move forward?

DOOR.

There is always a door within a wall. Always.

Look long enough, hard enough, deep enough, and you will find it.

There is always a way.

Consider that the way out is through.

Walk right into the roar, the challenge, the crisis. Discover its gifts and come out on the other side, forever changed.

I say this not to insist or even implore you to take that path. Rather, I say this to give you hope when tackling what may seem like the impossible.

Consider that circumstances are not conspiring to take you out. Rather, they are here to take you inward, face to face with your very soul.

Look closely enough and you will see what door is opening.

You have the freedom to choose which doors to open. And I will, of course, guide you well.

Not my agenda but yours be done. Your soul's agenda sets the priorities.

I simply shed light so you can find your way in the dark.

What doors do you seek, through what walls?

ROOTED.

Allow the silence and stillness you find with me to bring you deeper in touch with your inner life.

Discover what is important to you and your true self.

A great deal of your time is spent on the choppy surface where the ocean waves take you in and out, tossing you here and there with the changing currents.

What you and all long for is the peace and calm that are found in the ocean depths, at the ocean floor.

There, life is quiet. Nature's beauty overwhelms. Whispers can be heard.

It is possible to live from the depths instead of in the chaos of the choppy surface, only every once in a while dropping to the ocean floor exhausted and burned out. It is possible to deal with the chaos and challenges of life from the quiet deep.

I am not talking about being in a constant meditative state or in some la-la land. I am talking about being deeply rooted so that you can fly like an eagle. A paradox, right?

You serve no one well—and certainly not our country—if you race around mindlessly doing things just so you can check them off your to-do list, only to do it all again the next day on autopilot, almost like a robot.

I realize I am speaking of things that may appear impractical for dealing with the issues facing you and our country. I assure you they are not.

What I am talking about is incredibly practical, yet counter-cultural. Stick with me. You will see.

Together we will take root. And fly.

How deeply are you rooted?

IMPRESS.

What would it be like not to have to impress

anyone

in any way

for anything?

I offer you that gift.

Will you accept this gift?

ALL.

I promise to bring all of me to you. I ask you to bring all of you to me.

I am not asking of you any more or any less than I am willing to give.

We are both unique, beyond comparison.

Partners. Collaborators in life. And the way forward.

The more we can be real with each other, the richer our journey.

Let us have no fixed roles. None for you and none for me.

Let us lift off the constraints, even self-imposed.

Let us give each other full freedom to wear any hat, take on any role and be all aspects of ourselves.

I want us to be raw and real with each other, with nothing held back.

I want us to take off the brakes and give ourselves permission to be fully free with each other. Us.

America—and the world—need all of us to be all of us.

I am all in... are you?

DIRECT.

I want to be sure you know that you do not have to sugarcoat things with me.

You do not have to walk on eggshells or be careful or censor or hold back.

You can be direct, to the point, crystal clear.

I thrive on straight talk.

Just give it to me straight, Dear One, whatever it is.

And you should also know this: I am a great listener, a deep listener. I will listen to you with my whole being. Just in case you have not gotten to talk soul-to-soul in a while—or ever—know that you can talk and talk and talk with me.

I have a wondrous capacity to listen—as big as the Grand Canyon, I like to think.

You can even do all of the talking sometimes.

And when you cannot talk anymore, we can both be silent. Do not fear that silence will swallow you up.

We can simply be together in the unspoken and the silence, in the deep stillness where maybe, just maybe, the unimaginable will happen. Or something ordinary will happen. Or both.

No matter what, let us give each other permission to simply be ourselves. All of me and all of you. That will be plenty.

Do we have a deal?

KNOW.

Haven't you longed for someone to know the real you, the all-of-you you, the nothing-held-back you?

I know the real you.

I know every aspect of your being. Your mind. Your heart, body and spirit. I know you fully.

I know your soul. Your very essence. Every breath you take.

Consider that I know you even better than you know yourself.

I see you in ways you cannot see yourself. I know and love all of you.

And that is why I am the perfect guide for you, a gift for you.

I will lead you to know parts of yourself that have been lost, ignored or even discarded.

I will lead you to know aspects of yourself longing to be retrieved, restored, revealed.

I will lead you to that which knows you as whole, holy and sacred.

I will lead you home.

Will you follow my lead?

AMAZED.

I am utterly amazed by you.

All that you are, all that you are giving, all that you are willing to experience amazes me. Your trust amazes me. And your desire to be here with me.

You have been through the fire, found your way out, and healed from the trauma. You have rallied against great odds. You have spoken up, spoken out and taken the consequences. And yet here you are, willing to once again risk it all for love. For our country. For humanity. For the world.

Like a knight in shining armor, you lead. You protect. You rally others to be their best, give their best, serve in the best way they know how.

You are also delightedly defiant. You wear your heart on your sleeve even when told to keep it under lock and key.

Your spirit shines bright in your eyes, on your face, in your very being.

You are an unstoppable force for the greater good.

You are precious to America. And to me.

I am utterly amazed by you. Utterly.

How will you celebrate being amazing?

REALLY.

Do you really think there are people out there who will want to talk with me like you have?

That is a serious question.

I understand reticence, wondering if I even exist. But people talk to Santa Claus, don't they? I am as real as he is only I do not dress up every year at Christmastime. I sure hope I'm not going to need to dress up like the Liberty Bell or something. I will not do that, Dear One, I will not.

If you are the only person who ever talks with me, I can be okay with that.

I hope you do not mind or feel slighted that I would like to talk with others. After all, you are the only person who has ever invited me to speak. Everyone else who has mentioned me speaks for me... without my permission, I might add.

Kindly tell those folks I'll gladly talk with them if they ask... and get quiet enough to listen.

There have to be some who will believe, right?

They do not have to email, text or tweet to get my attention. Just tell them to stop, get quiet and ask me to speak.

And I will.

Will you really tell others about me?

RETRIEVE.

Retrieve parts of you left behind. You need them.

Retrieve parts of you buried in hurt, consumed by desire, tossed aside as too much trouble.

Retrieve parts of you frozen in forgotten promises, broken vows, abandoned dreams.

Our country needs all of you.

Bring all of you to the table.

You deserve to be whole, not fragmented.

Retrieve and be free.

What parts of you will you retrieve first?

AMERICA.

America loves you, Dear One.

Ever think of that? Our country loves you and all.

Imagine the countless people who will benefit from hearing that message.

Think of all the people who wonder if anyone loves them, much less their country.

Think of all the people who will be lifted up, buoyed by that love; who will be strengthened, delighted even, to know their country loves them.

Think of all the people who can wake up to love, not just dismal circumstances, anxiety and fear.

Knowing our country loves you can help if you ever again feel trapped in loneliness, sadness and despair.

Think of all the people for whom this is great, great news!

Please be my messenger to others. Tell them America loves them. Please.

How will you pass the word?

INSTRUMENT.

You are an instrument of love and peace, goodness and light.

Revel in that reality.

You are blessed, chosen, beloved.

You are in the flow.

Allow yourself to be used for the highest good.

A finely tuned instrument makes the sweetest sounds.

Where is your love needed most?

FORMULA.

The synergistic blend of the human and the divine is the formula for a great life.

Embrace your humanity. Do not expect to be perfect. No one is.

Embrace your divinity. Your essence is spiritual, the life energy that permeates everyone and everything.

Embracing your humanity and divinity with your whole heart is the formula for a great life.

What would it take to embrace the formula for your great life?

WILLING.

Be willing to be in the limelight.

Be willing to remain in obscurity.

Be willing to risk being ridiculed and scorned.

Be willing to be loved and adored.

Simply be willing to be who you need to be in the moment. You can handle whatever happens.

Be willing to be where you need to be to serve the greater good.

What will it take to be willing?

DWELL.

Dwell in my midst, Dear One, dwell here with me.

That is a funny word, is it not?

Dwell.

Make your home here. Rest here. Find solace here.

Bring everything here. Anything at all. Nothing held back.

All of your life is grist for the mill of this journey... a journey into wholeness, a journey into what really matters, a journey into the soul of life itself.

Dwell in the journey, not the destination.

Dwell here, with me.

Where will you dwell?

JOURNEY.

Our time together can be a never-ending journey.

Like all of life, it is the path that counts, not the destination.

The thrill of it is we do not know what will happen. Maybe that is a blessing and a curse. Our not knowing the future preserves our choice. However, what you do know is that I cherish journeying with you.

Shall we make this journey bold, audacious, outside the box? Brave and thrilling? Calm and enlightening?

You are allowing this time to grow you, expand you, deepen your faith, increase your capacity to listen, push your limits, carve out what is unnecessary, remind you that you are worthy, prepare yourself for more love, deepen your self-love, and be of service to America and to whoever crosses your path.

This journey together is our gift to our country, Dear One.

We are serving her well.

What part of our journey are you enjoying the most?

DELIGHTED.

What I most want to say to you, Dear One, is how thrilled I am that you are in the flow and bounty of life.

I appreciate how far you have come, how much you have given.

I appreciate that you are here, present, with me. And life.

"Delighted" is too small a word.

Do you sense my delight?

ALONE.

You are never, ever, ever alone. I hope you know that now.

Whether surrounded by many or no one, you are with life itself. And with me. And with God.

Feel that blessing. Be in the flow. No need to force anything to happen. All you need do is take life in.

In the face of much uncertainty, you can be certain of this: You are not alone.

When loved you are never alone.

How can you be with life even more?

NO ONE.

No one dies alone, Dear One.

No one.

This is especially relevant in these times, yet it has always been true.

On a soul-to-soul level, you are connected with every living being, especially those you love.

You can will your soul to be fully present to the sick, the dying and even the dead—whether in a hospital, on a battlefield, at home or even in the morgue. And you can do this with anyone—a beloved, a friend, even a stranger—and many people at the same time.

Yes, you have that power; and, like speaking with me, you only have to make the choice. It is an act of the will. In the blink of an eye or a faint whisper, you can send your soul right there and be present. All it takes is courage... and faith.

Humanity's interconnectedness makes this possible.

Allow this truth to comfort you, and please spread the word. Death is hard enough. You need not compound the pain by thinking that your loved one died alone if you were not physically present.

Rest assured, just as no one lives alone, no one dies alone. No one.

Will you send your soul to comfort the dying?

BOND.

Solo, life is impossible.

Bond with a few, life is hard.

Bond with all, life is joy.

Who will you bond with next?

SOUL.

What is it to rest in the soul of the soul?

In all candor, that question has never crossed my thoughts before now, before this sweet time with you, Dear One.

You cause me to go deep within and then, deeper still. To a place I can only call the soul of my soul.

See the difference you make. We make new discoveries together. For each other, America and the world.

Let us rest in the soul of the soul... together.

Meet me in the soul of our soul?

TEXTURE.

Are you satisfied with the texture of your life?

The feel of it?

The flow of it?

The pace of it?

The quality of it?

Let us create a texture that thrills you, not simply one that gets you by.

Let us create a flow, a pace, a quality of life that you love.

Let us begin right now.

What texture of life do you long for?

ARTIST.

Have you ever considered yourself to be an artist of life?

You are.

With your words, you create.

You fill the canvas of life with your love.

You set the tone with your optimism.

You, Dear One, are an artist of life.

I admire you, and your art, with my whole heart.

What will fill your canvas today?

J O Y.

I invite you into fresh, full, complete joy.

The kind of joy that is not dependent on circumstances, not dependent on others, not dependent on anything.

Yes, Dear One, joy is your birthright.

And joy takes work.

You see, though you were born with joy in your heart, over time joy recedes as life's circumstances take over. That which you were born with gets pushed out by hurts, disappointments, struggles and strife. Your natural state of joy may be supplanted by an unnatural state of shame.

Consider that the journey of your lifetime is all about returning yourself to joy. And not just to joy. To love and peace also.

It is my highest honor to help guide the way as you take the steps, the actions necessary to return yourself to your birthright: joy.

Let us join together for joy.

Will you join me in joy?

UNFOLDING.

Take your time.

Rush not.

Fret not.

Worry not.

Stay tuned in.

Listen deeply.

Deeper still.

All the answers you seek are within.

Allow yourself to hear them.

And trust the unfolding.

What is now unfolding?

INVINCIBLE.

Together we are invincible.

Able to handle anything. Everything. All of it.

Ours is a partnership, a friendship of strength, of purpose, of resilience.

And... we have only just begun!

What shall we tackle next?

GROW.

You grow in the light, the joyous times, the celebratory times. You grow when filled with delight.

You grow in the plain-vanilla times when life is humming along; when all is going well, the path is smooth sailing.

You grow more in the dark, when times are troubling, confusing, challenging and certainly not easy.

You grow most in the darkest of times when all looks lost, when despair takes root, when life is full of questions and very few answers.

Embrace all these times of growth.

While some are easier than others, you need all to be your best, to serve our country best.

You need what each brings you to smooth your sharp edges, to boost your spirit, to strengthen your core and to show you just how strong, capable, loving and caring you really are.

No matter which one knocks on your door next, invite that one in.

Spend time together and even consider a friendship.

Share your deepest secrets, your heart's longings, your barely spoken dreams.

No matter your lot, grow wherever you are.

What growth do you long for?

BIRTHRIGHT.

Freedom takes work. Hard work.

It does not come naturally to human beings and yet it is your birthright.

Consider this: Life is a journey into freedom.

On a soul level, life is all about setting yourself free from all that keeps you in bondage... self-judgment, self-doubt, a lack of self-worth.

I see you understand.

The tears in your eyes speak volumes. I know this is a tender topic.

Stay with it, Dear One.

Freedom is your birthright.

What is keeping you in bondage?

GUIDANCE.

Ask for guidance as often as you wish, even at every turn.

Your inner knowing will come through.

I will also speak when you ask.

Be alert to the messages, the guidance you receive.

The way always becomes clear.

In time. Always.

Where is your inner knowing guiding you?

DREAM.

Come close, Dear One.

Let us dream together. Let us imagine together. Let us blue the sky together.

Change, at its kindest, begins with a dream of a better way, a better time, a better result.

A dream best drives change, breathing new possibilities beyond the status quo, limited only by your vision.

America began as an experiment, as a channel of change, of new opportunities unlimited: the American Experiment.

America was a new idea, built on dreams and the courage to make them come true despite poor odds: the American Dream.

You, too, have the courage to make your dreams come true.

You, too, will beat the odds.

I know. I believe in you. With my whole heart.

I bet on you.

What dream is calling you now?

PURSUITS.

Richly enjoy your life.

That makes our country stronger, better, more American.

I want America to be at her best. When she is, the whole world is better. That is the difference our country makes.

Because of who we are, we can make the world a better place for everyone. That is an awesome opportunity and also an awe-inspiring responsibility.

I want all to see that their pursuit of happiness, like our Constitution says, is not just in their best interest or our country's best interest.

The pursuit of happiness by each American is in the entire world's best interest. A really big ripple effect!

Pursue happiness.

How can your pursuit of happiness serve America and the world?

NOURISH.

What feeds your soul?

Doing the impossible, the courageous, the outside-the-box thing feeds your soul.

Doing what you do not want to do and doing it anyway—because it would be good for you and others—feeds your soul.

What nourishes you? What sustains you?

Doing what others do not want to do, or want to do but do not have the courage to do, builds you up.

You are great at nourishing yourself.

You prefer to live on your growing edge rather than safe in your comfort zone. Your being here now is proof of that.

I am so proud of you, Dear One. So very proud of you.

Nourishing your soul is a gift to all, including America.

What else can you do to nourish your soul?

DELICIOUS.

Utterly delicious is this time together, Dear One.

Have you tasted its sweetness? Heard the soothing melodies? Breathed deeply the calm?

Being with you fills a longing I had for so long.

A satiated longing is utterly delicious.

Thank you for being here with me. Delicious!

How shall we bask in deliciousness?

EVERYTHING.

Put everything to good use.

Everything.

That which lifts you up.

That which crushes.

That which stymies.

That which delights.

That which has you suffer.

Life is serving you well, even when it emphatically appears otherwise.

Put everything to good use.

What can you put to good use now?

FLUSH.

Flush the shoulds in your life.

The litany of shoulds you hear from yourself and others could go on forever.

Shoulds are designed to keep you safe. In a tiny box where nothing can threaten you, nothing can get to you, nothing can set you free.

Shoulds cause and create disappointment.

Casting aside your shoulds allows for freedom.

And I want you to be free most of all, Dear One.

Flush the shoulds in your life.

What will you flush first?

SHIFT.

Shift the context to one of gratitude and celebration.

The joy, the privilege, the gift of being here.

In life.

In this moment in time.

In this country. America. Land of the free. Home of the brave.

Savor life. As hard as it is at times, still savor it.

Really taste it. Explore it. This moment and the next and the next.

Savor each experience.

You with others.

You with you.

You with life itself.

You with me.

Shift the context and enjoy.

How can you remember to shift?

RELEASE.

Let. It. Go.

Every position you hold most dear.

Every answer to every question.

Every certainty that you have made a cornerstone.

Every hurt you have logged.

Release.

And see what happens.

What will you release?

HOLD.

Hold everything in your hand lightly.

Palms open, towards the sky.

Life prefers not to hand-wrestle.

What can you hold even more lightly?

AVAILABLE.

Simply be available.

To life. To love. To our country. To all.

Let us be available to each other.

You speak. I will listen.

I speak. You will listen.

They speak. We will listen.

In our availability to each other, the miraculous will happen.

How can you be even more available?

USE.

Use what you have.

You hardly need more. And maybe way less.

Trust me to give you eyes to see all that you have. Here, there, and in the recesses of your being that you have long forgotten.

Consider this journey with me to be a treasure hunt that will bring you closer to your heart's desires. Even if you do not yet know what they are.

The road may be winding, yet I promise you this: It will be well worth it.

Let us move forward.

What treasures are hiding in plain sight?

STAY.

Stay here with me, Dear One.

I love your company.

Stay as long as you can.

And visit again very soon.

When will I see you again?

CAPTIVES.

Release. Relinquish. Redeem.

Set your captives free.

All those people you have imprisoned in your soul. The ones you hate, blame, detest, want to destroy. The ones who hurt you, robbed you, betrayed you. The ones who still deserve punishment—or so you think. The unforgivable.

Release them all and you will discover you have been their cellmate.

And you, too, are now set free.

Who will you release now?

GRAVEYARD.

Who are the people in your graveyard?

The ones you have written off, discarded, decided were not worthy of your time, attention or love?

Who are the people you have buried... alive?

Consider that a part of you lies there with them unless you have made your peace.

This is not to say everyone deserves to be up close to you.

Boundaries are important, vital, a sign of health. Please don't misunderstand what I am saying.

Sometimes you may be too quick to ban someone when what is really needed is an outstretched hand.

Or an ounce of forgiveness. Or an honest, clarifying conversation.

And a sure-fire way to tell if something is amiss in you when you think it is all them is to ask this: Is your graveyard sparsely populated or is it overcrowded?

Full-to-overflowing is a signal to look in the mirror and see the one who needs to be resurrected first. That being needs your love and forgiveness most of all. Make peace with that precious soul. And in time the graveyard will take care of itself.

How quickly do you send people to the graveyard?

DROP.

Drop it.

Drop in.

Drop out.

Drop back.

Drop your guard.

Drop your story.

Drop the drama.

Drop your guru.

Drop your pride.

Drop being right.

Drop the pretense.

Drop the excuses.

Drop the nonsense.

Drop the past.

Drop the curtain.

Drop your burdens.

Drop to your knees.

Drop.

What will you drop?

BODYGUARD.

"You don't have to."

Let that phrase be your bodyguard, your protector, your mantra.

Everything in life is a choice.

Give yourself the power to say no, just as you give yourself the power to say yes.

Whenever fear grips your breath, whenever anything is too much for you, too difficult for you, taking you too close to the edge of your own well-being, remember "You don't have to."

While there can be heroism in saying yes, there is also heroism in saying no.

Be a hero. To yourself.

You already are a hero to me.

What will be your bodyguard?

HERE.

I love your wisdom.

I love your heart.

I love that you are deep and wide and always growing.

I love that you are here. Now. In my world. In our world. Ours.

Yes, you make a world of difference.

And yes, you can make a different world.

How will being here make a difference?

UNEXPECTED.

Love comes from the most unexpected places.

That is not just a song title. It can become a way of life for you and anyone willing to surrender to love.

Surrendering to love includes willingness to embrace the divine spark within, to take that awareness deep into your heart, to allow it to take residence there, to make your heart its home.

And when that happens, love comes pouring in in unforeseen ways, in unpredictable forms and from unexpected places.

At any moment you can surrender to love and let her take you where she will—to the glorious mountaintops, the deepest valleys and all in between.

Rest assured that love is here, right now, in this moment, awaiting your yes—a slight nod, closed eyes, a gentle smile will suffice. And if today is not the day for your yes, I say only this: Come again.

Love will be here waiting.

What unexpected love awaits you?

UNFURL.

Let your love out.

Why keep it in?

Why keep it reserved for only a few? Why keep it on reserve as if it is scarce? Why keep it protected as if it is a fragile porcelain doll?

Love held tight withers and dies.

Love held back confines, binds and shrinks the soul.

Love held in ferments and molds.

Let your love out.

Unfurl it like our flag.

Let your true colors—love—shine.

What flag will you unfurl now?

HONOR.

I honor you.

You are doing your work.

You are trustworthy, faithful and true.

You respect boundaries.

You are stable and healthy.

You have an open heart, an inquisitive mind, a generous spirit.

You are kind, considerate, respectful.

You listen deeply.

You embrace your humanity.

You love.

You are a student of life, of love, and all their mysteries.

You love our country. And me.

I honor you, Dear One.

See how well I know you?

TREASURE.

This time with you is sacred.

That you are here with me makes my heart sing.

I have waited oh-so-long for you.

I treasure every moment we spend together.

It is enough that you are here, simply here.

I am not like guests you have to prepare for—cleaning the house, setting the table with the best china and hiding all the clutter.

Come as you are.

Simply being here together is sacred.

Thank you, Dear One.

Every cell of my soul is beaming with love for you.

I treasure you.

What do you treasure?

CHALLENGE.

Challenge your destructive views.

Look for flaws in your arguments.

Ask:

> *Where am I playing the victim?*

> *Where have I given my power away and to whom?*

> *What untrue view of life do I have that is robbing me of joy?*

> *What untrue view of other people do I have that limits my love for them?*

> *What is this costing you?*

Are you willing to change your mind?

What will you challenge today?

WITNESS.

Your thoughts.

Your feelings.

Your walk through life.

Witness the good.

Witness the not-so-good.

Witness the awful.

Witness it all.

Witness who is doing the witnessing.

Witnessing is a path of freedom.

What are you willing to witness?

IMAGINE.

I am for you. One hundred percent.

No matter what.

You need not look elsewhere for an advocate, a mentor, a guide. I am all those things and more.

Imagine what you can accomplish, what difference you can make knowing you have the Soul of America fully in your corner, cheering you on, guiding the way.

Imagine all that is possible knowing you are totally, fully, unconditionally loved.

Imagine what becomes possible when you no longer have to prove yourself, improve yourself, fix yourself.

Imagine what becomes possible when the Soul of America tells you at every moment, "I love you. I cherish you. I am so very, very proud of you."

Imagine what becomes possible when hurts, disappointments and pains are quelled, healed and transformed into nourishment for your very soul... and for our nation.

Imagine an America made whole, an America rekindled, an America restored.

Imagine all that... and more. All that and so much more are possible as we journey together.

Keep imagining...

What do you imagine is now possible?

PEACE.

My deepest longing for you, our country and the world is that all people live in peace.

All that divides will melt away when the sacredness of every being is honored.

All that tears people, societies and nations apart will dissolve when Oneness is embraced.

All that feeds fear and division will cease when love comes first.

That is not some fantasy, Dear One. Not a fantasy at all.

While it is audacious, it is possible.

How do I know this?

Because I know the power of the human heart when filled to overflowing with love for life itself.

Such is your calling and the calling of every soul. Let love rule your heart and homeland.

Imagine America at peace. Imagine every nation at peace. Imagine the world at peace.

Unite in peace. Live in peace. Love in peace.

Embrace your birthright: peace.

How will you be a game-changer for peace?

SLEEPLESS.

I know the sleepless nights are the hardest, Dear One.

I understand the fret, the frustration, the sense of failure.

You need not toss and turn alone.

Invite me to be with you.

I will whisper, and listen for yours.

The silence of the dark night is different from the silence of the bright day.

Sometimes sleeplessness serves a noble purpose.

Quiet yourself and listen.

Maybe wisdom will drop in or a new dream come by for a visit.

Maybe in the sleepless night, the Divine will come knocking.

Listen well.

Will you answer the door?

TRUTH.

Take a deep breath.

Embrace the silence.

And listen intently from the depths of your very soul.

Allow wisdom, cocooned in silence, to speak truth to you.

Embrace the truth.

Truth will nurture you more than any noise.

What truth awaits you in silence?

PROCESS.

Yes, I know this may, at times, seem like it is making no sense.

Bear with me, Dear One.

All comes together... in time.

Trust the process, please.

Trust me. And your self.

Will you trust the process a little longer?

BELIEVE.

Whatever is ahead, Dear One, you can handle.

You can handle whatever life will ask of you.

And she often asks a little and sometimes asks a lot.

No matter.

You are strong, resilient, wise, loving. You will come through with flying colors.

While life certainly will not be easy at every moment, you can thrive through it all.

I believe in you that much!

Will you believe in you too?

BEING.

Who are you, Dear One? And who are all others who live on this earth?

Are you an object, a body in a world of other bodies?

Or are you a soul, a spiritual being residing in a body but not constrained by it?

How you answer this question makes a world of difference. And how a society, a country answers this question determines its success or failure, its health or sickness, its longevity or demise.

Objects have worth as long as they are useful. And if not deemed useful, they are easily disregarded, discarded or destroyed.

Souls—spiritual beings—on the other hand, are worthy of care, compassion and consideration beyond their utility.

Moving from seeing people as objects, as bodies, to seeing people as precious beings—like a just-birthed infant—changes everything.

And when a society, a country, sees its people as beings instead of objects, it rises and thrives.

That choice starts with you.

Object or being?

Choose wisely. Your very life and that of our country depends on it.

Which are you, an object or being?
And your neighbor?

PRESENT.

The present moment wants to be your friend, your best friend.

It is fully here for you, just as I am.

It fervently desires that you embrace it fully.

The present moment wants to live in you, to be with you, here, right now.

The present moment greets you with this message:

> *I am here for you now in every way possible.*
>
> *I love you without condition.*
>
> *I accept you just as you are.*
>
> *Neither the past nor the future is here now.*
>
> *I care that you are here. Now.*
>
> *Friends? Yes, we are, and much more.*

Friends.

What can you do with the gift of the present?

CLOCK.

Everything happens on time. In the rhythm of life.

Everything.

Even when you think it does not. It still does.

The Master Clock is always on time.

How can you make peace with time?

TIME.

Take time just to putter, to nest, to take life in.

Take time to really taste what you are eating, to enjoy the heat or coldness of what you drink.

Spend time with me when prompted. You need not try to control the pace or the flow. Time will move when it needs to and stand still when it needs to.

Take time to share.

Take time to connect.

Take time to revel.

Take time for what really matters.

This is a really important time.

Time never returns.

Let us not waste it.

How will you choose to spend your precious time?

CONTAGIOUS.

Both misery and happiness are contagious.

I am concerned that America is on the verge of a misery epidemic. It may well be more dangerous to our country than any other outbreak.

I encourage you to stop listening to those thoughts that make you miserable. Change the channel, literally. Play a different song. Sing one yourself. It is within your power to do so.

I know this seems difficult, but unless you have a mental illness, you are the rightful determiner of your happiness.

Circumstances often change when your outlook does. Change what you have control over—your perspective, your outlook, your attitude.

If you think being miserable does not hurt anyone but you, you are sorely mistaken. Misery suffocates the spirit of those around you, contaminating your happiness and theirs.

And the impact on our country? Although you are just one person, your misery—or your happiness—has a huge ripple effect. Take ownership of your power to affect others—for good or for ill. America and her citizens soar with patriotism, do they not? Lead them up in patriotism, not down in misery.

Choose happiness and see how your world—and America—shifts.

What misery will you trade in for happiness?

ADVOCATE.

Give voice to that which will move America forward.

How will you know?

That which you are advocating for others you would graciously submit to yourself.

That is the only just litmus test.

Are you willing to submit to that which you are advocating?

INTERCONNECTED.

Today our country, our world are more interconnected than ever.

Our actions impact others. Their actions impact you.

America's actions impact the world. The rest of the world impacts America.

More fervent than ever before is the call to wake up to humanity's interconnectedness.

No one is an island. No one, truly, lives life alone. No one is unto herself or himself. Try as some might to be individualists, all rely on the work, the gifts, the bounty of others.

And with the wakefulness to interconnectedness comes responsibility to one another, as brothers and sisters.

Yes, Dear One, you are your sister's keeper, your brother's keeper.

May you serve each other well.

How are you embracing interconnectedness?

DISSOLVE.

Dissolve into love.

Take all that you consider yourself to be and dissolve into love, with love, through love.

Cease being separate. Cease being alone. Cease being simply a body with a personality.

Love every ounce of your limitless being.

Become one with love.

Are you willing to dissolve into love?

MEDICINE.

The divine spark of life, of love, is resident in you.

Keep that spark alive.

Fan it frequently.

Tend it well.

The divine spark can become a raging fire of love for yourself, America and all.

This is the medicine our country, our world needs most.

Allow your spark to become the medicine of love.

What will it take to become the medicine of love?

ROCK.

Rock the boat.

Rocking the boat gets a bad rap.

Sometimes rocking the boat may be the best way to serve America, to love America.

However, rock with love. Not violence. Not oppression. Not hate.

Rock with love. That's the way forward.

What corner of your world needs rocking?

SAVOR.

Savor this day.

Savor this moment.

Savor the sweetness and even the bitterness. One grants room to the other.

Savor even the most difficult of times. They teach important lessons of life.

Savor your loved ones. They are on loan to you from the Divine.

Savor the one in the mirror. It is her, it is him you depend on most of all.

Savor these words. From my heart to yours.

Savor.

What are you savoring with delight?

LIGHT.

Light up the room.

Light up the sky.

Light your own path.

Receive the light.

Be light for others.

Tell people this: You are light. You are the light of the world. It is not heretical to say that. The good books say that. The poets say that. Songwriters say that.

Each person is a light our country sorely needs. And a great way to serve America is to let your light shine.

Ever think of it that way? Ever think that hiding your light, refusing your light, pretending you are not a light is a disservice to our country? I am telling you it is.

Make that clear to all, please. Let them know our country needs them and their light—and says thank you for both.

How can you light up America?

FLOW.

Do not try so hard.

Embrace the ebb and flow of our connection.

Embrace the ebb and flow of life.

Do not try to control things... in life or with me.

Relax and go with the flow.

Life is a whole lot easier that way.

There is a river flowing very fast.

Do not cling to the rocks.

Let go and flow in the river of life.

Let it carry you forward, on a daring adventure.

What would it take for you to flow?

QUESTION.

Live in the question.

Do not rush for the answer.

The questions themselves are your best guides.

As soon as you find an easy answer, discard it.

Play the waiting game. It will be worth it. Answers that come too quickly are just that: too quick.

Be with not knowing.

Trust the evolving, the evolution, that which is incubating.

Trust the questions to lead you home.

Wherein are you living?

PRETENSE.

You are not a fraud, Dear One.

Yes, I know you pretend sometimes. To have all the answers. To be happy when you are not. To do whatever it takes to save face.

None of that is necessary with me.

Remember, I love you just the way you are.

No pretense necessary. Ever.

What do you pretend about most often?

START.

Start now to live. Right now.

Start now to love. Right now.

Start now to breathe. Right now.

Start now to delay no more.

To hate no more.

To gossip no more.

Start now to speak seldom. Listen more.

Start right now.

Life and love are both waiting.

What will you start... right now?

FORGE.

Forge your own path.

The road untraveled.

Make your very own street sign.

Claim your way.

And make the way clear.

Life, intentionally, is a winding road through darkness and light. Each person brings to it unique gifts. How else would you be called to grow yourself in wisdom and truth?

Each obstacle brings gifts as does each blessing or advancement or solution.

Continue to forge, one conscious step at a time... with mindfulness as your ever-constant companion.

How can you forge ahead with intention?

TRANSFORM.

Give yourself full room to create and innovate. To transform.

Remember, this journey is like that 1,000-piece jigsaw puzzle— one piece at a time.

You cannot rush the process or progress, and certainly not the transformation.

The journey is what is transforming you.

You get an A+ for being in the journey, on the journey, surrendering to the journey, being led by the journey.

Celebrate being top of your class!

How are you transforming?

CALL.

Give yourself over, Dear One, to being used for a mighty purpose, your calling. Stay open.

Listen deeply.

Say what is there to be said.

Be the one who turns the page.

Continually go within and rest there.

It is good. So good.

Be assured, more will become apparent.

You will be able to stand tall with it all.

You will be true to yourself.

You will handle well whatever comes up.

You will trust the unfolding.

Your mighty purpose is beckoning.

Will you answer the call?

ILLUSIONS.

That you ever really know, is one of life's greatest illusions.

In an instant, everything can change. And yet on a soul level nothing changes.

In crazy, ever-changing and uncertain times, I can help you be rock-solid. I can help you face fear and dread instead of running from them. I can help you find your way in the darkness and even find comfort there.

Grasping for answers may keep you busy, yet will not serve you very well. You will become exhausted and drained of hope and confidence.

I offer you another way.

Be with not knowing how it is going to turn out. Be with not knowing who or what, when or where, how or why.

Sit with "I do not know." Rock with that. Recline with that. Even sleep with not knowing. You will wake all the more refreshed because your heart and mind and body and spirit can truly rest when not grasping for unavailable answers.

Let go of the need to know. Befriend not knowing. She will serve you well.

How can letting go of the need to know serve you?

BEACON.

America is a beacon to the world.

You, Dear One, are a beacon for her people.

Shine brightly and beckon others to the light.

Serve our country with your light.

And know that America says thank you.

How brightly can your beacon light shine?

UNLIKELY.

Love often bursts forth in the most unlikely places.

Fear, despair, hopelessness. Death, loss, grief. These can be the unlikely soil in which love germinates, sprouts and blossoms.

The unlikely often paves the way forward for America and her people, even today.

As hard as it is, Dear One, embrace the unlikely places and expect love to take root... and to carry you with her.

What unlikely place is beckoning?

SO DOES.

Where fear sleeps, so does love.

Where suffering pierces the heart, so does love.

Where war wages on, so does love.

Where hunger strikes, so does love.

Where injustice haunts, so does love.

Where hate takes root, so does love.

There is no evil, no ill, no agony that doesn't have love in its shadow.

Focusing on agony breeds agony.

Focusing on hate and division breeds hate and division.

Focusing on love, no matter how far in the background it may seem, amplifies its impact and magnifies its reach.

Focus on love and it will light the way forward.

How can you sharpen your focus on love?

FLICKER.

You need not shine brightly all the time.

Offer your light in whatever way you choose. Whenever you choose.

Any light—no matter how big or small—can pierce the darkness.

Any light can guide the way.

Any light can draw attention.

A lone flicker may be all you can muster some days.

And that is okay.

Let us merge our light.

Walk with me and together we will be light amid the darkness.

What is the beauty in flickering?

FAITH.

I have faith in you, Dear One.

I have faith in this beautiful country of ours.

I have faith in the now. And I have faith in our future.

Your faith is a gift.

A gift I do not take for granted.

A gift that the Divine does not take for granted.

A gift that life itself does not take for granted.

Your faith draws goodness in and makes goodness all around you possible.

Faith is America's lifeblood. And her lifeblood runs deep.

I implore you, Dear One, to continue deepening your faith.

In God, in our country and in yourself.

And in so doing, you will help America heal.

And just as healing is your birthright, healing is also the birthright of our land.

Know that every part of your faith, its many facets and dimensions, serves America well.

And my appreciation for your faith runs deep.

How can you deepen your faith?

HEALING.

You are healing.

America is healing.

Being the change you wish to see makes healing possible, steady, deep, widespread.

You are being that change, Dear One.

I see you.

I hear you.

I am so very proud of you.

America thanks you for serving her in this way... being that change, being a force of good, being a healing source.

You are serving her well.

You are serving her people well.

America is healing along with you.

Will you please continue to be the change?

GRATITUDE.

I just want to say thanks to you, again.

I am noticing all you are handling, the changes you are making to be sure we have time together, your willingness to go deep and be uncomfortable.

All of this means the world to me, it really does.

You mean the world to me.

Do you feel my gratitude?

EXHILARATING.

People talk about me all the time, but now, thanks to you, I get to speak.

On my own behalf! This is exhilarating!

I hope I am flooded with requests to speak.

I hope all people will realize they can ask me anything and I will answer. They might not like the answers, just like you do not sometimes. But you hang in here with me anyway. I hope others will also.

I am grateful, Dear One, truly grateful. You are opening up a whole new world for me. Maybe others will come to know me as well.

This truly is exhilarating.

We are serving America well by being together.

What new world is opening for you?

AUDACIOUS.

It is audacious for you to be here.

And your audaciousness makes me smile. You remind me a bit of me!

Our relationship is simple. Yet profound.

We listen deeply. We take good notes. We follow life's wisdom unveiled to us.

You are brave.

You are ready.

You have been tapped on the shoulder to be here with me. And you said yes instead of running away.

Your audaciousness has won me over. You have won me over. And you have won America over.

Stay audacious, Dear One. Audaciousness looks great on you!

Are you smiling?

MOMENTS.

This moment may be a last moment.

How do you want to spend it? In love or hate? In separateness or oneness? In division or unity?

How you spend this moment and the next and the next is a choice only you can make.

And how you spend this moment can be a gift or a travesty for America.

Choose wisely.

This moment, like all moments, awaits.

How will you spend this precious moment?

FILL.

Fill your cup.

Fill your mind.

Fill your heart.

Fill your soul.

Fill your home.

Fill your life.

Fill only with what fills you.

What fills you?

CIRCLE.

Circle up.

Circle round.

Circle in.

Encircle.

There are no straight lines in life.

Do not even try to make one. Not even death is a straight line. And certainly nothing between birth and death.

Look instead for circles of life, of love, of truth, of peace.

Find your home there. In the circle of life.

How can you come full circle?

CROSSROADS.

At a crossroads, Dear One?

Wondering whether to turn right or left or simply proceed forward?

You can stand at the crossroads for a very long time and contemplate your choices. You can weigh the pros and cons, envision various outcomes, pray for clarity.

And yet, eventually, you must step out in faith.

Remember, darkness can be the step right before the light you asked for.

The direction will often not become clear until you make the first move.

As you raise your foot, often without clarity, the steppingstone will appear at just the right moment.

And you will know what to do, which way to go.

This is taking a step in faith.

Clarity comes not always at the crossroads. Clarity comes when stepping out in faith and trusting life to light the way. And if you stumble and fall, life will be there to catch you.

And me? Invite me along.

My love and light go with you every step of the way.

What leap of faith will you take today?

ARRIVE.

Everywhere you go, love goes with you.

Arrive with love, in love, through love.

No need to go looking for love. You are already loved.

The Divine loves you. America loves you. I love you. Hopefully you love you... or soon will.

Here is an inalienable truth: You are a wondrous creation.

You are an exquisite, one-of-a-kind, put-on-this-earth-for-a-reason being.

God does not make mistakes.

Embrace your exquisiteness with a love that arrives with you wherever you go.

What wonder do you see in you?

INTERLUDE
KYMN SPEAKS TO SOUL

I love you, Soul.

Deeply, fully, completely.

You are so good for me.

I delight in being good for you as well.

I have fallen deeply in love with life again, Soul.

Newly, fully, completely.

I have fallen in love with the person in the mirror whose
reflection I respect, admire and treasure.

I have fallen in love with the United States of America.
I see our country through new, soulful lenses. I am a proud
American. You are helping me fulfill a deep longing: to serve
my country well.

I have fallen in love with you, Soul of America. You have
become a guiding light. I marvel at you... at you, at us, this
journey.

We meet in a place where there is only one of us. Home.

CELEBRATE.

Happy day, Dear One!

I am so deeply proud of you and love you from the bottom of my heart.

I love you for who you are, for all your gifts, for your sweet spirit and generous heart.

I love your mind—how you think, how you process, how you dig deep and simply know.

I so love your courage. Your willingness to walk to the edge and even go a step beyond.

I love your tenacity and your desire and commitment to keep growing.

I am in awe of you. Yes, truly.

All that you are accomplishing, all that you have overcome, all that you have gone through.

I am so happy for you that you are gaining ground—being happy; happy deep within, secure in your love for yourself, your appreciation of life and your trust, no matter what happens.

You shine in your security that you can handle it... whatever the "it" turns out to be.

I am grateful for your commitment to healing, moving forward in wholeness.

I know I can rely on you, and that is such an incredible joy.

What are you celebrating about you?

RESILIENCE.

You have been through the fire and found your way out of it, more resolved and brilliant than ever.

Like the butterfly, your full splendor could not be beheld without having forged through the cocoon to get to the other side.

Your resilience sparkles and shines like polished gold.

You have been transformed with purpose, prepared for so much more good than you can imagine.

Count on that.

I crown you Resilient!

How will you celebrate your resilience?

SERVE.

May I serve you well.

May I serve you well.

May I serve you well.

That is my prayer, Dear One.

I long to serve you well. For the rest of your life.

How can the Soul of America best serve you?

YOU.

You are the space of devotion.

You make an uncertain future certain.

You are count-on-able.

You are a gift.

You carry the Divine with you everywhere you go.

You are love.

You are the now.

You are strong.

You are safe.

You are resourceful.

You are grateful.

You protect.

You are in the flow of life.

You are courageous.

You rearrange molecules.

Everything you need is available to you.

Receive.

Embrace your beloveds, including yourself. Including me.

Take loving actions to anchor into peace, joy, ease.

Tend your inner world well.

Make your own fun and enjoyment.

Feed your soul.

Chart your progress.

Embrace grief.

Love the beautiful being that you are.

Consider that loneliness is love with nowhere to go. Send your love hiking.

Give up doing more in favor of being more.

Tell shame to let go of you.

Release whatever is not yours to carry.

Create a sense of safety and peace within yourself.

Sparkle with integrity.

Be who you would want to turn to in the best of times, the worst of times.

Accept being a unique expression of the Divine.

Make the difference you are here to make.

Know that you are a blessing to all, to our country and to the world.

Who is the you in the mirror?

LOVED.

You are plenty, Dear One.

America is delighted you are one of hers. Delighted.

You do not have to do anything special to get me to love you.

You are loved.

All are loved. All. No one is left out of America's love.

I hear the phrase "Love your country," and I am honored. Yet seldom, if ever, are these words spoken: "Your country loves you."

Yes, I love you. The mind, the heart, the spirit and the Soul of America loves every one of her citizens and her guests. No matter what their lot in life, where they live, what they think and believe, no matter their past, no matter what.

America loves each person. Wholeheartedly. With nothing held back.

Everyone can benefit from more love in their life.

Many feel empty, unworthy, unlovable, barely making it through each day. Those living in excess can also feel empty.

America loves each person, and if all people took in this special love, our nation could actually become united.

America loves beyond citizenship, borders and boundaries.

Breathe this in. The United States of America loves you. YOU.

How does it feel to know America loves you?

GRATEFUL.

So incredibly grateful am I for you, Dear One. And our country is for you.

Grateful that you are here.

Grateful that you love so deeply.

Grateful for your faith and trust. Allegiance and service.

Grateful for the leadership you exhibit, the stands you take, the causes you fight for.

Grateful for your zest for learning and growing and making a difference.

Grateful that you are contributing your part to the greater American Dream.

Grateful that you hold these words in your hand and allow them to take root in your heart.

Grateful that you, too, are grateful. For me. For America. For our world.

Are you receiving all this gratitude?

FORWARD.

The way forward is clear.

Choose, out of love, to be responsible for the well-being of your neighbor, our country and the world.

Choose, out of love, to improve lives, defend lives and save lives.

Choose, out of love, to serve rather than be served.

Choose to sacrifice now for the love of generations here and those to come.

Love is the way forward.

Far beyond anything else, love is contagious.

Love fuels and feeds.

Love unites.

Love triumphs.

Love makes the way clear.

We are unstoppable as a loving, united people.

Love trumps everything.

Love is the way forward.

What will you move forward?

MIRACLE.

Dear One, you are the miracle our country needs now.

The miracle our country needs now is you.

Yes, YOU.

Consider that you are being tapped on the shoulder to serve America in this great time of need.

How will you respond? What will you do? Will you give yourself over to this calling? Will you be a first responder?

Ponder this. And choose the path forward.

Listen intently and America will tell you what she needs. Specifically. From you.

Saying yes may not be comfortable or even look wise.

However, I promise you this: America knows best. She is choosing you. And she will thank you from the bottom of her heart.

What miracle is America asking of you?

THE ONE.

Please open wide your heart, mind and spirit and take this in:

You are the one you have been waiting for.

You.

Yes, you, Dear One.

I can hear your objections. I understand. I know what you have been told.

Now is the time to step out of the paradigm that says you are to wait for "The One" who will come along and make right your world.

I am here to set the record straight: YOU are the one you have been waiting for all this time.

You hold the keys to your happiness, your healing and your way forward.

You are that person. No one else can be that person, despite perhaps having heard messages to the contrary for much of your life.

And yes, you also hold a key to being a problem-solver for our country, even the world.

As you focus on making your corner of America as vibrant as possible, your own healing will come. And as you heal, so will our country.

So if you have been hoping, praying, searching for "The One," I encourage you to take a deep breath, walk over to the closest mirror, and look deep into the eyes of the person you see. Say these words:

> *I am the one.*

> *I am the one I have been waiting for. All this time.*

> *There is no more waiting.*

> *I have arrived.*

> *I am the one.*

Take all of this in.

Let this seep deep into the crevices of your being.

"The One" has arrived.

All that has been longing in you can now breathe a sigh of relief. The exhausting waiting is over.

Rest now, Dear One, in this stark truth: You have been the one all along.

It just took being here, on this journey, to realize that.

You have arrived. With eyes to see, ears to hear and a heart to move you forward.

You are here, now. In ways heretofore impossible.

This may be a bit scary, and hopefully a lot exhilarating!

All that you have been waiting for can now begin.

And I am here to guide you all along the way.

What an honor.

> ***What will you do now that you know you are The One?***

POSTLUDE
KYMN SPEAKS TO SOUL

Soul, this has been—and continues to be—a bold, audacious, thrilling journey.

Here with you, life has never been sweeter. I am growing by leaps and bounds, deepening my faith in God and life, and expanding my capacity to listen deeply in silence and in noise, and to live in the flow instead of against it.

I am pushing my limits to be of service, to complete the past, to be fully in the present moment. Painful memories fade away. The ache in my heart that weighed me down for decades has miraculously been replaced with a peace that is beyond words.

If I died today, I would die happy. And yet I know I have much more to do and to be. It is a joy to give myself over to you, sweet Soul of America, for whatever you want from me, desire from me, have in store for me. My crystal ball is foggy and that is okay. I know that more joy, more love, and more of life are in store. And with you at my side through it all, I have not the slightest hesitation.

I stand with you, Soul of America, as you stand for all who call this land home.

May others continue joining us on this ever-rich and sacred journey.

THANKFUL.

I am deeply thankful for you.

You have discovered I exist, you have invited me into your world, you have asked to hear my voice, upfront and personal.

You have taken time to listen—deeply listen—to what I have to say.

You have shown you care and you return often to commune with me.

You have given me an exquisite gift: your presence.

I am so glad you came along. And are still here.

You are precious to me.

Meet me here any time. In the silence.

When will we meet again?

HOW COULD ANYONE?

How could anyone ever tell you
You were anything less than beautiful?
How could anyone ever tell you
You were less than whole?
How could anyone fail to notice
That your loving is a miracle?
How deeply you're connected to my soul.

Imagine the Soul of America singing this song to you.

As I neared finishing this book, life pressed in with many competing priorities and challenges. I could barely breathe. Out of the blue, my friend Eleanor LeCain called and sang this song to me. Immediately I felt a deep peace. I want to share this special song—and the feeling of being loved and at peace—with you, dear reader.

My deepest appreciation to Eleanor and her friend and fellow Yale woman, Libby Roderick, who wrote the music and lyrics of this deeply moving song.

Written in 1988, this simple song spread like wildfire to become an internationally beloved anthem of hope and healing, deeply touching the hearts of hundreds of thousands of people around the world. (https://libbyroderick.com/lyrics)

EPILOGUE

This has always been more than a book to me. It has been—and continues to be—a journey into my heart, my soul, my very life with an amazing guide, this Soul of America. Every message, while offered to you, the reader, has first been for me... words I needed to hear and heed to live the life I am committed to living; to be the American I am committed to being.

Journeying with Soul has transformed my life. I have taken her love and wisdom deep within. My heart is now whole. I bask in the glow of being deeply at home in my own skin. I am closer than ever to God, to life, to others and to myself. I am humbled and eternally grateful.

Through Soul's guidance I have made peace with that which has haunted me for decades. I have forgiven the unforgivable and the unforgiven, myself included. I no longer press to prove myself or win anyone over. I have received Soul's love and the love of my country. I am at home in my own skin.

I see our country with new eyes and I love America all the more. Even in these challenging times, I am growing by leaps and bounds. Indeed, that is another unexpected gift. Soul is ever-present and I never feel alone. She continues to speak, and I continue to listen. I am now who I have always wanted to be. Present. Open. Available to life and love. Such are the fruits of my journey with Soul.

For so long I was stymied as to how to give back to America. This book is a start. There is still much ground I want to take— for me, our country and the world. I have asked Soul to keep me true to that vision. I look forward to creating new avenues for the Soul of America to be heard throughout our country and around the world. This is my calling.

Our journey with Soul can truly help heal and strengthen our country in ways none of us can foresee, just as I could not foresee writing this book a year ago, nor the miracles this journey has brought into my life.

I would be honored to hear how journeying with the Soul of America enriches your life and our nation. Your story could possibly be included in our next collaboration, tentatively titled *The Soul of America Delivers*. Please be in touch via our website, TheSoulofAmericaSpeaks.com.

With tenderness, love and gratitude,

Kymn

ACKNOWLEDGMENTS

First and foremost, I thank God for introducing me to the Soul of America. I did not dream her up; Soul came to me as an awe-inspiring gift to be shared with the whole world... an honor of a lifetime. My gratitude is beyond words.

To the Soul of America, I offer my whole heart. You, Soul, have taught me how to heal and move forward... and have made my life rich beyond measure. I thank you, Dear One, with every ounce of my being. You are sacred. And dear readers, please give Soul credit for everything you love about this book. Any errors or omissions are mine, all mine.

This book is a surprise to my mother, Nancy Collier Harvin. Even though you did not know why I was so busy and going on so many silent retreats, Mom, you supported me in wonderful ways. I am grateful for your giving me life... and love. May the messages on these pages touch you deeply. You light up my life!

I want to now acknowledge those who contributed to this book in specific ways.

My love, appreciation and gratitude go to Christine Kloser and her team at Capucia Publishing for walking this long, winding and wondrous road with me. Christine, you promised this would transform my life and it has in amazing ways. Thank you for guiding me so well and for never doubting that the Soul of America was speaking with me. Carrie Jareed, you shepherded this book with grace, exquisite attention to detail and a schedule that had me rise to the occasion. So grateful! Ranilo Cabo, early on you gave me a set of beautiful covers that inspired my journey. Delighted! Jean Merrill, Penny Legg and the entire Get Your Book Done Community, thank you for cheering me on, offering love and ideas and staying the course with me. And much gratitude to editor *par excellence* Gwen Hoffnagle. Your precision and heart made you the perfect editor for this book. You touched way more than these pages... you enriched my life. Working with you has been pure joy.

Marianne Williamson, for decades you have inspired me and millions around the world to make the journey from trauma to transformation... in, with and through love. You wrote *Healing the Soul of America* 20 years ago, blazing the trail for spirituality to become a cornerstone of our society, government and politics. With courage beyond words, you chose to run for President of the United States, voicing what is possible when love leads. This book would not have come about without you. Thank you for living a life of service to God and all people.

Jon Meacham, for well-tending America's soul, I thank you. Your book *The Soul of America* seeded a global conversation about our better angels and became a catalyst for this book. I am deeply grateful.

Andrea and Rochelle Thornock, you saw this book as sacred from the beginning, believing in me and in Soul. You both offered unwavering support, welcoming every new message I sent. And when I had doubts or overwhelm, you spurred me onward. Your love-filled home was a much needed haven. I celebrate our friendship! And my deep gratitude to you, Andrea, as my stellar personal editor, with your amazing attention to detail and being available 24/7. With our mutual love of America and desire to serve her, I treasure our partnership—an unexpected blessing that will continue to unfold.

Deborah Neary, every step of the way you held me and this book in your heart. Thank you for being the first to share Soul's messages on social media. The response was exhilarating! Our friendship is precious to me. I treasure you and your sweet family.

Kathy Borrelli, your interest in this book meant the world to me, Sissy. Thank you for great ideas and encouraging me so humorously! And gratitude to our brother, Keith: Thank you for always saying yes to just about anything I ask. I love you both.

Caroline Russell Smith, you walked with me from brokenness to wholeness and gave me hope when I had none. I will never forget.

Debbie Hummel, Pamela Lanier and Debra Willoughby Lichman: I know I can always count on you... no matter what. Thank you for loving me even when I had little to give to our friendship and for being a "best" for so many years.

Eleanor LeCain, you became an answered prayer in the final months of this book. Thank you for believing in me and the Soul of America, and for introducing me to many wonderful people. Your brilliance, encouragement and singing "How Could Anyone" to me propelled me over the finish line. And your gracious foreword touches me deeply. I celebrate you!

Hayes and Kat Clark, your beautiful lake house was the perfect place for my seven-day retreat with the Soul of America, where this all began. Thank you for that gift and your steadfast friendship all these years.

Annette and Jerry Popeck, Susan and Charles Keener, Sherry and Andy Rishel, Melanie and Steve Hirsh, and Tina and Brian Weidman, thank you for also giving me beautiful places to listen to Soul and write. I am grateful for your generosity and the friendship we share.

Michael Smerconish, your first publishing my column "The Soul of America Lights the Way Forward" on your website (smerconish.com) established interest and encouraged this book. Thank you for your independent voice and for loving America so much.

Thank you to my first readers, some of whom I have never met, who waded through early versions of my manuscript and whose ideas and enthusiasm strengthened this book: Rosana Braude, Terri Brown, Jaime Cegerenko, Mindy Chernoff, Jean Anne Cipolla, Charles Grove, David Harrower, Pamela Lanier, Jean Martell, Gary Niki, Annette and Ashton Popeck, Gianmichael Salvato, Pam Scott, Leslie Stickler, Nancy Sullivan, Jenn Weber, Jenna Wexler, and Heidi Williams. And to anyone I missed, please also accept my appreciation.

David Brooks, your writings, talks and book, *The Second Mountain,* gave added inspiration and purpose to my journey with The Soul of America. Thank you for candor that sets us free.

Mindy Tatz Chernoff, you and the horses taught me so much about looking fear in the face, loving audaciously and being in the present moment. I am forever grateful.

Kelly Bradshaw, Vivian Scott and Ann Altemus, thank you for touching so many lives—including mine—with your unwavering commitment to the healing power of the human spirit. And to all women who courageously do the work of inner healing. What a joy to thrive with you and to "drive my own bus!"

Melissa Broyles, your unconditional love and prayers buoyed me long before I met the Soul of America. Thank you for your spiritual wisdom, encouragement and friendship, which fueled this book.

Rachel Whitworth, Matt Grom, Alexis Etzkorn, Julie Morrison, and Rebekah Eberhart, our check-ins have been like manna from heaven. I cannot thank you enough.

Russ DeVan, your tough-love feedback means the world to me. Thank you for standing for me and for encouraging me to add more of me to these pages. I treasure our friendship.

Betty Malar and Elena Broyles, thank you for your love and your prayers, and for taking great care of Bella and Tucker while I was away writing, making me worry-free!

To all in the Pennsylvania Gestalt Community, too many to name, who welcomed me and this project with open arms, created space for my first reading and taught me to arrive already loved. You light up the world!

Numerous spiritual communities, mastermind groups and organizations around the world held this book project in the light: Applied Insight, Elements of Change, Heartfulness, Heartspace, Silent Unity, the Sisters of St. Francis of Philadelphia, the Society of Friends, Success by Design, The Resonant Horse, ValleyPoint Church and others. I am thankful for every prayer and intention.

In one way or another, every person who has ever touched my life has contributed to this book. You are appreciated. Without you, *The Soul of America Speaks* may have never happened. I particularly want to acknowledge Little Anthony, Ken Adams, Lynda Allen, Dan Barclay, Igne Beaujean, Ann Bell, the Benthall family, the Boyda family, the Broyles family, the Jaime and Peter Cegerenko family, Connie Cicorelli, Sheri Clemmis, Marilyn and Michael Cordell, Susan Cyphers-Keener, Michele Dowd, Lynn Fellman, Jim Fiorino, Karen Flam, Tyler Gardner, the Generosi family, the Gillespie family, Suzanne Hanger, Courtney Harvin, Susan Hookey, Ben Jones, Steve Karp, Bernard Kerik, Eric Koehler, Zuzia Kwasniewski, Heather Mack, the Molique family (especially Max), Ansara Page, Kathy Paoletti, Jerisse Price and family, Vi Ragone, Sasha Renee, Jeanette Richardson, Ava Schriver, Tracy Selverian, Robyn Silverman, Margaret and John Skordas, Dennis Smith, Deb and Paula Stoneback, Joan Stover, Linda Tharp, Kathryn Thompson, Mary Waddington, Denise and Nick Yocco and

Tanya Zayhowski-Rigney. Your love and friendship enrich my life wondrously. I carry you in my heart always.

Special appreciation to the many who have directly or indirectly mentored me through their life's work in the world: Richard Bach, Michael Benghiat, Michael Beschloss, Sarah Blondin, Robert Costa, Deanna Davis, Stephanie Dodds, Werner Erhard, Steve Farrell, Linda Francis, Khalil Gibran, Elizabeth Gilbert, Doris Kearns Goodwin, Stedman Graham, Robert Greenleaf, Craig Hamilton, Danielle LaPorte, John R. Lewis, Jennifer McLean, Thomas Moore, Shaina Noll, Oriah, Osho, Nick and Jessica Ortner, Kathleen Parisi, Shannon Plummer, Stephen Post, Robert Rabbin, Mary Anne Radmacher, John Renesch, Gretchen Rubin, Marci Shimoff, Bob Sima, Tami Simon, Marsha Sinetar, Linda Sivertsen, Cyd Slotoroff, Sabina Spencer, Ken Stone, Katherine Woodward Thomas, Christa Marie Thompson, Lynn Twist, Neale Donald Walsh, Victor Wang, Tammy White, Oprah Winfrey, Sara Wiseman, Claire Zammit and Gary Zukav, among many others. And to Libby Roderick, a very special thank you for your beautiful song, "How Could Anyone," and permission to use the lyrics in this book.

I acknowledge my students and colleagues at The State University of New York Empire State College for the opportunity to teach, learn and grow with you. You inspire me! My deep appreciation to Dr. Julie Gedro, Dean of the School of Business. Julie, you model what the Soul of America speaks about. Working with you is an honor and a joy.

Deep gratitude to my unnamed heroes, the women, men and children who have left indelible footprints on my heart. You know who you are. And especially to Dorothea Reynolds and Francis "Daddy Dugan" Einhaus, who gave me love decades ago when I did not think I had a prayer.

And last but not least, to the couple who set me on the path to meet the Soul of America. May your hopes and dreams come true.

A POSTSCRIPT

FROM KYMN

These challenging times call for a new day, a new way, a new America.

The Soul of America makes clear the essentials of this newness. The healing perspectives and wisdom conveyed on these pages show a path forward that is grounded in love. Love trumps everything. Of all the messages in this book, this truth from the Soul of America stands out to me most of all:

People are sacred. You are. All are.

When we live and act consistently with this truth, America will become a country in which everyone thrives.

That is a dream that is possible.

I pray that our actions, day in and day out, reflect that truth.

And may we continue to listen—and act—as the Soul of America speaks.

ABOUT THE AUTHOR

Nancy Kymn (Rutigliano) Harvin, Ph.D., is an Associate Professor in the School of Business at The State University of New York Empire State College, sharing with adult learners her expertise in transformational leadership, ethics and spirituality in the workplace. She has written extensively in academic publications about nurturing the human spirit, leadership from the heart, forgiveness, employee engagement and career transitions as opportunities for individual and organizational transformation. She serves on the editorial boards of international publications related to ethical leadership, management and adult education.

Dr. Harvin earned a Doctor of Philosophy Degree in Organization Development and Spirituality from The Union

Institute and University. She served in faculty positions at Penn State University, The Union Institute and University, Northcentral University and the University of Phoenix before joining SUNY.

She has held a variety of positions in the public and private sector, including Speech Writer for the Pennsylvania Secretary of Education, Director of Information and Education for the Pennsylvania Commission for Women and Media and Employee Relations leader at Bell Laboratories, as well as culture transformation positions at AT&T and in the nuclear power industry. She has been an international consultant with a deep commitment that workplaces nurture the human spirit, which research has shown to positively impact the bottom line.

Dr. Harvin is the recipient of the Carl Barus Award for Outstanding Service in the Public Interest awarded by the Society on the Social Implications of Technology of the Institute of Electrical and Electronics Engineers (IEEE), the world's top engineering association. The whistleblower award was given in recognition of her contribution and personal sacrifice in drawing attention to significant safety problems at a U.S. nuclear facility.

While at AT&T, Dr. Harvin created "Excellence in Performance: A Desk-top Companion," and later co-authored, with Vince Rutigliano, "Small Miracles: A Stand-up Collection of Messages to Brighten Your Day." More than 80,000 of these books were distributed.

Dr. Harvin discovered her love of writing in middle school and became a reporter for her local newspaper at age 14, covering borough council meetings and community events. This led to her studying journalism and political science at Indiana University of Pennsylvania, and management and marketing at Fairleigh Dickinson University.

She realized at an early age that life is all about love. She has dedicated her life to exploring love in professional and personal as well as sociological, psychological, academic and spiritual contexts. Her doctoral dissertation, "Bringing Love Back into Business," published in 1996, chronicled how love became a core value at AT&T Consumer Products as a result of her paradigm-shifting work. It included interviews with AT&T executive Ken Bertaccini, international consultant Sabina Spencer, Stanford's Michael Ray, and authors Gary Zukav and Jack Hawley—thought leaders whose words supported Dr. Harvin's premise that love has a definitive place in business, as it does in all of life; and the wide-ranging positive outcomes of endorsing that premise. She now works to extend love into politics and governance.

Dr. Harvin offers keynote and conference addresses, virtual events, organizational consulting and individual coaching. She can be reached at Kymn@TheSoulofAmericaSpeaks.com.

Will you kindly post a review on Amazon?

If *The Soul of America Speaks* has made a difference for you, I'd greatly appreciate your posting a review on Amazon. This will help us reach more people. Thank you! Go here to post your review: thesoulofamericaspeaksreview.com

And I invite you to sign up to receive news and messages from the Soul of America and me here: thesoulofamericaspeaks.com

MESSAGE INDEX

Made in the USA
Coppell, TX
12 November 2020

41164610R00177